A MORAY LOON

A MORAY LOON

BY
STEWART ALAN ROBERTSON

WITH AN INTRODUCTION BY
T. HENDERSON

THE MORAY PRESS
EDINBURGH & LONDON

First Edition 1933

EDINBURGH : GRANT & MURRAY, LTD., 126 PRINCES STREET
LONDON : 39 PARKER STREET

Printed in Great Britain by The Riverside Press Limited, Edinburgh

The papers in this collection have appeared from time to time in THE SCOTSMAN, THE GLASGOW HERALD *and* THE SCOTTISH EDUCATIONAL JOURNAL, *and they are reprinted with the kind permission of the Editors.*

Introduction ◔ ◔ ◔ ◔

STEWART ALAN ROBERTSON was born at Loanhead,
Midlothian, on 25th April 1866, and died in
Edinburgh on 23rd January 1933.

Like so many Scots of his generation, he went
straight from his landward school (at Lasswade) to
the University of Edinburgh, where he graduated
in 1888, with honours in Philosophy. He was an
eident, ardent youth, and won many distinctions,
notably in the subjects of English and Education,
to both of which he dedicated his working life. A
fortunate appointment to a Travelling Scholarship
led him to France for the purpose of reporting upon
the educational systems and methods of that
country. His sojourn there left a deep and per-
manent impress on his mind. For the rest of his life
he was a fervently wholehearted upholder of the
Auld Alliance. It is a matter of great regret that
his period of leisure from official work was not
sufficiently prolonged for him to weave the many
strands of Franco-Scottish connection into an
ordered history, as had been his ambition. Few
men were better equipped for so delightful a work.

When he returned from France, bringing with
him much more than his official baggage of
information concerning schools and colleges, he was
appointed assistant to Professor S. S. Laurie, *nomen
venerabile*. Thereafter he taught in Edinburgh and
Stirling for sixteen years before going to Croydon
as Chief Inspector to the Education Committee, a
post he held for other sixteen years, for ten of

which he was also Adviser to the Education Committee of Wimbledon, ere he returned to Scotland as Director of Education to the City of Dundee in 1920. He retired on reaching the age-limit in 1931.

The record looks honourable but unexciting, yet it is simple truth to say that many hundreds of pupils and teachers found in his fellowship during these years, inspiration, help and stimulation, and if the revelation of the qualities that evoked these responses does not entitle a man to rank among the high adventurers, it is difficult to imagine how so proud a title can rightly be gained. Over and over again it has been said that the teacher's chief reward is the loving recollection he calls up in the hearts and minds of his pupils. If that be so, no man was ever so rich as Stewart Alan Robertson. Wherever his old pupils meet, his name is the most frequently mentioned, always with deep affection. The most remarkable tribute of all is the way in which their talk turns to the lessons he taught them. English was the nominal subject, but somehow or other to them, looking backward, it seems that the whole art of life was embodied in those gay, wise, incomparable hours they spent with him. None was so poor in mental endowment as to gain nothing from his unceasing interest in the working of children's minds, his inexhaustible resourcefulness in illustration and his passionate regard for the right to free development of each of the human personalities in his care. No doubt some gained more than others, but all gained much, for he kept the Latin counsel ever in mind—*Maxima reverentia pueris debetur.*

He was a Scot of the old lineage. None ever better combined the granitic quality of the race with the romance, the waywardness, the glamorous poetry that, call it what we will, is an essential ingredient of the true Scot. His was the Scotland that lies at the Back of the North Wind, the Scotland that claims with pride as its sons both John Knox and the Ettrick Shepherd.

He was the least taciturn of men, though he could be taciturn, like all wise men, on occasion. But in the proper company, and there were few companies into which he did not fit easily, he was the king among them a'. His wide and curious reading, his French experiences, his devotion to the land of his fathers, his whimsical humour and his unaffected interest in all things human, made him one of the most delightful of companions. He certainly found great happiness in his work as an administrator in Education, but it is possible that a fitter sphere for him would have been a Professorship of English (or Scots) Literature, where his perennial youth would have touched the life of later generations to finer issues.

The heavy demands of official business compelled his writing to assume a slight and apparently fugitive manner. Distinction it always had—it sparkled and warmed, like some of the wines of France. But in reality nearly all his writing is linked together, diverse though the topics may be, by the dominant interests of his life. Scotland and, next to Scotland, France were his themes. Though born in the Lowlands, he was proud of a Highland ancestry on both sides. He loved to revisit the Robertsons' country of Rannoch and the Stewarts' home in Appin. He loved France deeply for her own sake, but chiefly, I think, because History had bound the two countries together. He made the best of both his worlds. He was at one and the same time a stern Covenanter and a follower of Joan of Arc. He retained to the end certain Gallicisms of aspect—a free swing of the shoulders, a jaunty perching of his hat, a coquettish up-turn of the moustache, and a livelier mode of utterance than is common in Scotland. The Auld Alliance was a living reality to him, and the terrible years of the War confirmed him in his double allegiance. Once I ventured to propound the heretical doctrine that German poetry fell more pleasantly than French on a Scottish ear, and appealed more surely to a Scottish mind. I remember still the expression of horror with which he retorted that no country whose place-names were such harsh explosions of cacophony as " Ehrenbreitstein " could ever hope to compete for the poet's laurels with a nation that could coin such melodious place-names as " Vaucouleurs." But his France was like his Scotland—a land of age-old memories, deep-rooted friendships and scenes of immortal loveliness.

This little volume has brought together a few of his essays on the subjects that attracted him. It is the merest handful of examples from a treasure-house that all who knew him regarded as inexhaustible. It is hoped that it may be regarded as a memorial, slight but of precious material, to one whose passing darkened life for very many; to one who had a genius for friendship and gave fully and without reserve of the riches of his personality.

T. H.

Contents

Patrick Geddes ◇ ◇ ◇

PATRICK GEDDES was the most seminal Scottish mind of the last fifty years. His vibrant intelligence shot forth ideas, projects, theories, as some plants eject their spores. He should have been kept like the queen bee in a hive, with swarms of worker-bees to put into practice the visions of his fertile brain. No Scottish professor for half-a-century has been so widely known among the *intelligentsia* of France, Germany, Italy, America and Hindustan. Yet this great Scotsman held in Scotland no post higher than the Chair of Botany in University College, Dundee. Nor had any Scottish University honoured itself by enrolling him among its honorary graduates. He died as he had lived, unhooded and ungowned, belittled in his last days by the knighthood that is available to any pushful politician or provost.

Forty years ago, multitudes of young men in Scotland and in England owed their souls to the teaching of Patrick Geddes. In those days of Darwinian determinism, Grant Allen's sad lines seemed incontrovertible :

> *A crowned Caprice is the god of this world,*
> *On his stony breast are his white wings furled.*

Even a noble soul like Huxley could see in life essentially "a gladiators' show." Geddes, pupil of Huxley, challenged the verdict in his books, in his lectures, in the flood of vivacious speech which leaped from him like a fountain. I recall the thrill which went through an audience as Geddes

A   I

traced the basal feature of all life to be the sacrifice of the mother for the offspring, and closed by saying, with the usual fingering of the abundant locks and the phrase over the shoulder, " So life is not really a gladiators' show, it is rather—a vast mothers' meeting." Such biological teaching rallied young minds to faith in the rationality of the universe, in the possibility of progress, in the value of life, in the triumph of justice and truth, if men would but search widely, think deeply, and, above all, labour together for the common gain. No man was more brotherly than Geddes. When the University Court of Edinburgh gave me a grant to visit schools in France, Professor Laurie said to me: " Go and see Pat Geddes, he knows all about France." If I had been his youngest brother, he could not have been more generous with advice and introductions. He sponsored me to the Quartier Latin. He gave me an introduction to M. Compayre, then at Poitiers, whose *Histoire des Doctrines de l'Education* was the only scholarly work of the kind until Sir John Adams wrote his *History of Educational Theory*. He gave me a letter to Madame Kergomard, who showed me Les Ecoles Maternelles, which cared for the little ones of Paris before the name Nursery School was heard. Through Professor Geddes I came to know M. Pécaut, principal of the Training College at Fontenay-aux-Roses, a philosopher of the type of Malebranche, Cousin, Bergson, and I was visited by the Marquis de Vaneuil, whose carriage and pair made a great stir before my *hôtel garni* in the Rue de l'Ecole de Médecine, in which Charlotte Corday murdered Marat. The Marquis and Geddes had become allies through a common devotion to the doctrines of Le Play, the sociologist who was Geddes's master. I had never even heard of Le Play, though I came to know full well in later years the work of Le Play House in

London. According to Geddes's exposition of Le Play, the concept of race as physiologically determined is an error. Race is a culture-concept, the two chief factors of which are occupation and geographical conditions. Men's minds are moulded by climate and features of earth and air and sea and by their bread-winning. "But," as Geddes would say, "you must make your geography a geosophy." He had a gift for *le mot juste*. But he was sometimes in danger of being satisfied with the word, and would give a description as an explanation. Still more did he love a diagram, rather an ideograph. Give him a piece of chalk, set him before a blackboard and all the history of the world, all the knowledge of man, all the marvel of the future, would be represented in symbols. That characteristic is shown in the Outlook Tower in Edinburgh. You pass from its base, which represents primeval man with his curtailed outlook, up through successive storeys, symbolic of successive ages, and their gradually widening view, until you reach the summit. There the camera obscura reveals the world of to-day symbolized by Edinburgh throned between the mountains and the sea.

All things had a voice to the ear of Patrick Geddes; all their messages must be related to life, either in its Great Record of the Past or its Great Adventure of the Present. On a day at Culross, under his guidance, that slumberer since the seventeenth century would awake, and its forgotten life be enacted again. Some recall him most vividly in the days of the University Summer Meeting, of which the University in its academic formalism took no cognizance. They will recall him when he was introducing M. Elisée Reclus, geographer and sharer in the Paris Commune; or M. Desmoulins, whose " A quoi tient la supériorité des Anglo-Saxons " sounds ironical to-day; or Professor Rein, from Jena, who found, as Rousseau did, all the method of a good education in *Robinson Crusoe*. Others may remember best the rambles, the picnics, the receptions, which varied the lectures, when Geddes would explain why the theism of Mahomet could have been learned only on the plains of Arabia, or the relation between the pastoral conditions of Ireland and the tendency of its folk to be sweer to gree, or the resemblance between the labours of the medieval astrologers and the work of the insurance experts of to-day, or the absolute necessity to "orientate one's self" on reaching any strange place. So he poured forth vivacious, whimsical, wide-ranging, deep-searching talk, "de omni re scibili et de quibusdam aliis."

I thought him at his best as a lecturer when he was addressing the members of the Nature Study Association in London, and would relate all the range of education to a flower in the crannied wall. So also when he spoke to my teachers in Croydon on the interrelations of geography and history. He illustrated his thesis by reference to the Thames, with its English capital city, London, and its sacred place of coronation, Westminster, paralleled by the Tay with its Scottish capital, Perth, and its sacred place of coronation, Scone. As one listener said, Geddes at his best made one think of the lines in *Kubla Khan*:

> *For he on honey-dew hath fed*
> *And drunk the milk of Paradise.*

He could be dull and wordy, when the wheels seemed to have come off the chariots, so that they drave heavily. Once, when staying with me at Stirling, he bored a great audience with irrelevancies and inconsequences, and even confused Stirling Bridge with Lauder Bridge. Yet the same night, five men at a fireside were entranced by his talk about his experiences in Cyprus. Its progress depended, to his judgment, not on electoral reform, but on having a supply of new seeds and on knowing how Moses struck the rock. "The last fresh seeds were taken there by the Crusaders, and no grafts have been made on their fruit-trees since." "They could have a water supply if they would clear the channels which have been choked by the waters flowing over calcareous soils."

Geddes's best monument in Edinburgh is the pile of buildings which his enthusiasm raised around the Goose-Pie home of Allan Ramsay. Here is his reasoning for that work: "Scottish Universities give their students lectures, and take no concern with them beyond the class-room. That system may invigorate some, but it has destroyed many, and restricted most, and it is false to the final purpose of education, the fitting of man for a social activity. English universities err at the opposite extreme: they treat young men as schoolboys, whose exits and entrances are regulated, who move to a common code, who have no scope for learning self-government and who are moulded to a pattern of 'what is done.' In University Hall students will live a common life, which they themselves will manage. They will be drawn from all the faculties: medicals, arts men, engineers, budding ministers. Artists, advocates, schoolmasters, ministers, etc., etc., will dwell in the flats beside the students' hostel. Town and gown will give and take from each other width and comprehension. All will be affected by the historic site. And all will give time and thought to befriending and encouraging the less fortunate who dwell in adjacent closes." Since Amphion raised the wall of Thebes by his music, there has been nothing like the raising of University Hall by the eloquence of Patrick Geddes. University hostels are a commonplace nowadays. All can grow the flower now, for all have got the seed. But how great was the loss to the University of Edinburgh that it did not make itself partner in the Geddesian project. When Cecil Rhodes was contemplating his Foundation for the Rhodes Scholarships, he found that eight out of every dozen men in South Africa were graduates of the University of Edinburgh. He therefore included Edinburgh with Oxford and Cambridge as Universities at which the scholarships might be held. Learning later that there was no system of " internal residence " at Edinburgh, he withdrew the name of that University from the deed of foundation.

Only those who knew University Hall in its early days will agree that " bliss was it in those days to be alive." It was an adventure to climb the newel stair, where a rope took the place of a handrail, where each door of a flat bore the old Scots " risp," so that one " tirled at the pin " for entrance, as in the ballads. So one came to the ultimate flat, whence northern windows saw a ship tacking for The May, the Forth, and its isles, or at night the beckoning light from Inchkeith or Fidra, while the southern casement looked sheer down to where Lady Glamis was burned and out past the bulk of the Castle, with the window of the room in which Mary Stewart had her travail, to the green slopes of Caerketton and far Carnethy, flecked with the sheep which Stevenson's John Todd was herding. " The piper that played before Moses " welcomed you on entrance, and the Seasons were radiant on the inner walls. " You won't mind sitting on the floors, we're going to get more chairs when we have some more money." Thus does the charming voice of Mrs Geddes come to me over the years. Fiona Macleod was expected that evening, an author then in the bright halo of novelty and mystery, though a few were sharp enough to solve the enigma.

J. Arthur Thomson, whom some have described as Geddes's best achievement, was there, agreeable but taciturn, accumulating thereby the store of cadences, charming phrases, and deft allusions with which to delight his hearers and readers in the future. I was asked by Mrs Geddes to try to get him to talk more. What I remember most vividly is that we broke one of the fruit-plates between us.

University Hall of course included more than Ramsay Garden. I was always glad to be a guest of the students who harboured in Riddle's Court, in the house of Bailie Macmorran, whom a seventeenth-century High School boy pistolled when the magistrates tried to put down a "barring-out." The Bailie's saloon was a handsome room, and its panelled plaster ceiling bore the cipher of King James VI. and I. and the lion sejant, which was his crest.

Naturally there were features of the life at University Hall that offered scope for criticism. A rather satirical picture of its life and of Geddes himself appears in *The Cruciform Mark*, a novel which is true to the Edinburgh of the time, though spoiled, as so many books are to-day, by an irrelevant dabbling in the occult. The author was a Cornishman, attracted to Edinburgh by Geddes. It was always part of his philosophy to bring together all nations, so that the widest diversities might influence each other, or at least comprehend each other. There was a time when "Synthesis" was the magic word with Geddes. According to him, the cardinal evil of the nineteenth century was its individualism, personal and national, and the canker of its science and education was its especialism, in which one subject regarded not another, and ignored its relation to life. Geddes's gospel was that all studies should be interrelated and that all should converge towards securing a fuller, higher, corporate life. To vary the *Hudibras* line, "Geddes could not ope His mouth but out there flew a hope." He never despaired of the republic. Many in Edinburgh will recall the pageant which he directed. It was afterwards shown in London, he himself taking the part of Erasmus, if my memory serves me. It closed impressively on the great stairway of the Imperial Institute with a figure from an aeroplane foretelling the happiness of the years to come. How we all cheered! Within a year, the aeroplanes were whirring over Verdun. Even the War could not discourage Geddes, though it took from him his son Alasdair, a youth of rare promise, and though the German cruiser the *Goeben* sank the vessel which was taking out for exhibition in India his treasured collection from the Town Planning Exhibition in London.

People who were not attracted by Geddes's sociological theories admitted the practical value of his work for town-planning. He told me that his mind turned to town-planning because he had to live in Dundee, " a town with the finest site in Scotland, spoiled by the absence of a plan." He planned many wonderful possibilities for Edinburgh. In one of his books a photograph of the rear gardens of Charlotte Square, separated by walls into ugly strips, is juxtaposed to a photograph of the same area as a garden in common for all the indwellers. He showed me, in the London Exhibition, a plan for the rebuilding of College Street and Lothian Street as a series of students' hostels, thus connecting the College of King James with the School of Medicine. The picture rises before me every time I see the sordid reality. He had a project also for a terrace in front of the Assembly Hall, with a decorative stairway, such as one sees in Florence or Ferrara, to take the place of the brae that climbs to Ramsay Garden. There was talk at the time of a Carlyle Memorial in Edinburgh, and Geddes suggested that the monument should be placed on the terrace. I said to him: "You are not really much of an admirer of Carlyle." "No," he replied, "but I like bric-a-brac." That was true, and he loved colour. When he interested people in his project of a Co-operative Country House, where one would be assured for week-ends or holidays of good accommodation and a cultured *milieu*, he bought a charming house on the North Esk at Kevock, and at once set to having tiled roofs, balconies and dormer windows put in.

Could any but Patrick Geddes have moved Crosby Hall, the medieval mansion in Bishopsgate, London, in which Richard III. had dwelt, to Chelsea, that it might be the Common Room of a block of students' hostels beside Sir Thomas More's garden? He had in truth the faith that moves mountains.

There was something of the Scottish wandering scholar of the Middle Ages in Geddes. He was eager to purchase the Scots College in Paris to make it again the home of Scots who would share the cosmopolitan life of the Sorbonne as in the days of Abelard. No one could be more ardently a Scot, yet no one was ever less particularistic or Chauvinistic. "I wish to undo that evil result of the Reformation, the breaking of the intellectual unity of Europe," he once said to me. Yet he had only amazement and a quiet smile at people like M. Hilaire Belloc and Mr Chesterton, who imagine the vain thing of a restored medievalism. He did not much use the patois of the professional philosopher, but humanism, pragmatism, holism might claim him as their adherent.

There is no space to write of his books and pamphlets, but his effort as a publisher merits note. I have heard of a Scots Renaissance at least twenty times in the last forty years, and have heard many voices say, "Now here! now there." But the roseate hues of early dawn, how swift they fade away! The nearest to a real Renaissance was when " Patrick Geddes and Colleagues, in the Lawnmarket of Edinburgh," became publishers. They issued *The New Evergreen: a Northern Seasonal*, from the very spot where Allan Ramsay had sent out *The Evergreen*, which began the revival of Scots verse which gave Scotland Robert Fergusson and all that came after. Their publications, *The New Evergreen, Lyra Celtica*, the writings of Fiona Macleod, *The Interpreter*, were different from normal books in format, in typography, in binding, in illustration, in contents. No wonder one dreamed of an Edinburgh again recognized as the Modern Athens. The chief practical result of the enterprise was to send many Geddesians to study the art and legends of Gaelic and its cognate tongues, or to interest themselves in Provençal, so wonderfully revived by the poems of Mistral, or to practise rondeaus, triolets, villanelles, and discover Villon and Charles d'Orléans, whose rhythms had been the models of many a Scots makar for whom Dunbar lamented. Perhaps, after all, such is the true Renaissance, not a counterfeit of the past, but a widened present.

Geddes's last project was in harmony with all his schemes, and yet was true to *le dernier cri* of to-day. He had come to see that modern conditions make even a united Europe insufficient. He had no patience with the ideal of an Empire, regardless of all outwith its bounds, gazing, like Narcissus, in admiration of its own perfections. He dreamed of the World-State, like Mr Wells. But Mr Wells' conception of a World-State is Americo-European. It has efficiency as its chief aim. An enemy might call it Philistine. Geddes, though he looked West, did not forget to look East. He did not think that the differing civilizations and philosophies of China and Hindustan had been through the centuries but a murmur of gnats. So he maintained that the World-State must take account of the views of Orientals, who should be allowed to put their opinions, their hopes, their aims, in the pool. Only when studying together and living together for study do men reveal themselves fully or come to know each other intimately. What University might be the fit focus for such co-operation and such endeavours? Montpellier, the only European University which looks to the Mediterranean, that linkage of East and West; Montpellier, whose renowned medieval school was founded by Arab physicians; Montpellier, which had included as students Petrarch, Rabelais, De Candolle, De Jussieu, and even Clarendon and Locke. Geddes dreamed that the beam that shines from Montpellier Hill shall lighten every land. In every effort to gain " light, more light," Geddes felt Scotland must share. So he established at Montpellier the Collège des Écossais, where Scots might mingle with every race known under heaven, so would they aid the coming of the world of which Patrick Geddes dreamed.

Genesis xxxvii. 19: "And they said one to another, Behold this dreamer cometh. "

Genesis xli. 41: "And Pharaoh said unto Joseph, See, I have set thee over all the land of Egypt."

A Forgotten Scot ❧ ❧ ❧

EVERYONE knows Goldsmith's description of the Irish schoolmaster in *The Deserted Village*, and can quote the lines:

> *. . . And still the wonder grew*
> *That one small head could carry all he knew.*

There is no parallel picture of the Scots schoolmaster of the eighteenth century either in verse or prose. Sir Walter Scott approaches the subject in his sketches of Reuben Butler and Abel Sampson, his satirical portrait of Jedediah Cleishbotham, and his sympathetic kit-cat of Peter Pattieson, but he shies off from detailed treatment.

Once upon a time if anyone named Auchinleck to me I thought only of the mansion in Kyle to which James Boswell escorted Dr Johnson to meet his father's welcome. Had I used my little Gaelic, which tells me that the name means "the field of stones," I might have realized that the name would not be uncommon in Scotland, and I should not have been surprised to learn of Auchinleck Castle in Angus. Surprise begat curiosity which begat a visit which begat pleasure at seeing a well-preserved example of a sixteenth-century tower. It remains as when built in 1580, and its indwellers made no mark on history. It affords a better background to the imagination because it stirs no emotion by association with any dramatic incident or exciting personality. The conditions of life of a small laird in the days when Scotsmen ferlied at the tragedy of Fotheringay or whispered their uncertainties about the doings at Gowrie House are clearer as one stands in the hall of Auchinleck, or inspects its oratory, which still shows a piscina, a holy-water stoup, and an aumbry, or gazes at its " garderobes," from one of which the lady could survey her servants at work, herself unseen, or espy at a lower storey the approach of a visitor. At Auchinleck I understood, for the first time, what was " the grund wa' stane," by which " Jock, my man," in the ballad *Edom o' Gordon*, " let in the reek."

Auchinleck, usually shortened to Affleck, is in the parish of Monikie, formerly Eaglais-monaich-tigh— the church by the monk's house. It is undeniable that Celtic names have a euphony which the Teuton cannot match. Matthew Arnold felt this truth when he mourned that any human being should be named Wragg.

There is a flippant saying that it is not possible to throw a brick anywhere in Paisley without hitting at least three poets. It is at any rate true that every Scottish parish can cite some local writer, however forgotten and however " minimus." At Monikie I came to know about Alexander Balfour, who knew much about Scots schools of long ago and who might have filled the gap which I began by lamenting. His story is worth telling, were it only as another instance of that literary effort under conditions of bodily weakness for which Robert Louis Stevenson is honoured. Alexander Balfour was born at Monikie in 1767, and was engaged in the linen industry in one capacity or another in Arbroath, Dundee and Fife. From his youth he had been in the habit of contributing to journals and periodicals, and at the mature age of fifty-one he took service with Blackwood, the famous Edinburgh publisher, the founder of *Maga*. The next year, however, Balfour had a paralytic stroke, and the remaining ten years of his life may be compared

to those which Heine spent on his mattress-grave
in Paris. Yet in these years Balfour composed
several novels, much verse and many articles, and
was a minor planet in the starry sky of Edinburgh
a century ago. One cannot praise his verse, which
abounds in poetic diction, as if Burns had never
lived nor Wordsworth written his *Prefaces*. Here is
a stanza on spring flowers:

> See purpling orchis towering rise
>   Midst cowslips in the greensward vale ;
> While violets hid from mortal eyes
>   Breathe incense in the vernal gale.

He wrote a long poem with the title *Contemplation*,
which has almost "everything intil't." But it is
written in tripping trochees, after the mode of
Milton's *L'Allegro*, though its subjects would require
rather the slower movement of Cowper in *The Task*.
Balfour had much fluency, but lacked simplicity.
His Scots verse is neither Scots nor English!

> The snaw was deep, the wind was cauld,
>   And halflins past the winter day,
> As helpless, hameless, poor and auld,
>   A wanderer sought his weary way :
> His thin grey locks waved in the wind,
>   And mony a deep indented trace,
> That showed the world had been unkind,
>   Was marked upon his manly face.

The success of Crabbe's *Parish Register*, with its
description of rural folk, led Balfour to write similar
pieces, which he issued under the title, *Characters
Omitted from Crabbe's Parish Register*, and which were
often attributed to "Nature's stern painter but her
best."

Balfour wrote several novels: *The Foundling of
Glenthorne, Highland Mary, The Smugglers' Cave*, full
of thrilling but improbable incident, cinema-
scenarios before the cinema. He might have been
a rival to Galt if, like Galt at his best, he had written

of the world around him. He resembles Galt in parts of his novel *Campbell, the Scottish Probationer*, which occasionally touches on the schools of the time. It tells in autobiographical fashion the story of the only son of an Angus crofter. His mother and grandmother are eager that the boy should " wag his heid in a pu'pit," an ambition which the father opposes: " Deed, I see mair ministers than kirks. It needs moyen and gude freends to get a berth amang the clergy. Say noo the laddie's colleged and leecensed, what's he to dae till he gets a kirk? Hoo mony are there are fain to get the length o' a dominie and wring oot their lives in a parish school, a drudgery waur paid than mine. A three-bare coat and a toom wame mak but a bauch gentleman." The lad was colleged and licensed, but found no patron to present him to a kirk, and was glad to take a post as tutor in a laird's family. The daughter fell in love with the tutor, and told her love in an *Ode to a Wood Pigeon*:

> *Thrice happy bird, had I thy power*
> *To wing my flight to distant shores*
> *And nestle in some secret bower*
> *With him my aching heart adores.*

The tutor's heart throbbed similarly, but "imperious necessity required that I should immediately renounce my situation." Whereupon the maiden pined and died, and the tutor lived unhappy ever after.

Campbell's education had begun thus: " In my fourth year I was sent to a school in the village kept by an old maid. She taught English with a broad Scotch accent in the following order: the ABC, the Proverbs of Solomon, the New Testament, the Bible from Genesis to Malachi, always saving and excepting Chronicles and Nehemiah, which being, as she said, Latin, she did not profess to teach."

Thence he went to the parish school, where the

master was "a tolerable scholar and a good man. His greatest failing was indolence: he had no hopes to stimulate him; his character and situation in life were fixed; he saw himself condemned to vegetate and die in the same spot. Hence the ardour which he felt not himself he had ceased to excite in his pupils." There is shrewd insight in that description.

As no patron offered a kirk, Campbell opened near his home what was known as a Subscription School, a number of parents agreeing to contribute an annual salary of thirty pounds. He had difficulties with his pupils; he lacked patience for the teaching of the younger, while some of the elder loons resented his use of the tawse. The parents as paymasters thought that they should have a say in school matters. One father objected to his children being taught the Catechism, while the mother wished them to learn the Catechism "with the proofs thereof out of the Scriptures," while another would be satisfied only with the teaching of Willison's Mother's Catechism. Then the story was spread that the dominie was "a blackneb," or sympathizer with the Revolution in France, and he had to resign his post. Through the good offices of a friend he obtained a post as parish schoolmaster in another village. All went well for a time till Campbell refused to allow the time-honoured custom of cock-fighting in the school on Shrove Tuesday, Fastern's E'en. "I always endeavoured to address myself to my pupils' hearts as well as to their heads, and took every opportunity of instilling into their minds the principles of veracity, justice and mercy, forbidding acts of cruelty to any creature." It is clear that his dominie's mind rose above the cockieleekie which other teachers found acceptable and savoury.

After this passage of realism, Balfour sends his

hero to London, where he fell among thieves and had various adventures. But England was exile, and he took ship for home. " How often did I chide the winds for slumbering in their caverns as I viewed the sail flapping on the mast in my passage, and when the blue hills of my native land rose upon the horizon I wished for the wings of an eagle that I might reach the spot where my heart had long hovered."

Campbell's next application for a post as teacher was again to the managers of a Subscription School. He and a much younger applicant were asked to attend for examination. Campbell surpassed his rival in knowledge of Latin and mathematics, but one of the subscribers expressed himself as disappointed with Mr Campbell's pronunciation of the words, burial, revenue, plaid, and others, as " old-fashioned." " I have seven daughters," the complainer said, " and I am unalterably resolved that my daughters shall be taught in the newest, most fashionable, and approved style, method, and manner." Campbell was therefore set aside in favour of the younger applicant, who accented " revenue " on the first syllable and said " oblige " without betraying its relationship to the saying, " Noblesse oblige."

Campbell betook himself to Glasgow, which takes all accents to its kindly bosom, and for five years earned his bread as a students' " coach." The story closes with Campbell, at the age of seventy, retired to his native parish, supported by a small allowance from friends, and moralizing " that life will close in the most pleasing serenity which has been most actively employed for the welfare of society."

Archie ❦ ❦ ❦ ❦ ❦

" I SEE Archie Waterston's death in the papers."
" Aye, doon aboot London somewhere. He
hasna made muckle o't. He was never onything
but a curate, and him a B.D. Aye, Archie should
hae stuck to the teachin'."

Thus did two men of his native village comment
on Archie, whose story I would like to tell.

His boyhood's home might have made Archie a
poet, if environment were a determinant. It saw a
ruined castle rise above a noble sweep of a romantic
river in an amphitheatre of woods. Archie trudged
daily thence to a parish school of high repute
throughout Lothian and beyond. In due course he
became a pupil teacher and, as the high bicycle
had been devised, he could reach school at 8.15 A.M.,
to continue there till 5.15 P.M., with a briefer time
of transit. It was not much briefer, since half his
route was too steep to ride up and the other half
almost too steep to ride down. He taught Standard
IV. from nine o'clock till four, and had two hours
of lessons daily from the headmaster. He studied
English, Mathematics, French, Latin, Greek, with
an essay to write for every Monday and a map to
draw for every Thursday, and instruction in drawing for an hour twice a week from a visiting teacher.
Under her direction he copied sketches of Italian
contadinas and of the bridge over the Rhone at
Saint-Maurice. As a teacher he was more eager
than effective or lucid. So many thoughts arose
simultaneously in his mind that his words came,
as Rosalind wished Celia's words to come, " as wine

18

comes out of a narrow-mouthed bottle, either too much at once or none at all."

The system of concurrent attendance at a Training College and at a University had recently been established, and Archie's headmaster, a man of exceptional character and scholarship, made it his ambition that all his pupil teachers should be qualified for that double course. One had to secure at the Queen's Scholarship examination the significant letters, L, G, M, denoting excellence in Latin, Greek, Mathematics, before one could bind the double burden on one's back. Archie was successful in securing the "letters," and I recall vividly the day he came to school to say farewell on his way to the University. Archie off to College, his face radiant, with the bright eyes and dark hair—he had what used to be called a coo's lick— was something of a wonder to us juniors, especially as he carried the nodose walking-stick without which no University student of Victorian days went abroad.

The system of concurrent attendance was an advance, but it made a monstrous claim upon the strength of youth. For Archie, as for myself much later, it meant classes at one institution or the other from 9 A.M. to 5 P.M. There was no interval, a "piece" being swallowed as one hurried from a fifty-minutes lecture at the one to a fifty-minutes lecture at the other. Three men, who should have died hereafter, succumbed to the system in my time. Archie, coming from what was an exceptional school, was irritated at having to spend time at the Training College, listening to lecturers, whom he compared to their disadvantage with his head-master. He was showing himself of promise in Latin and Greek at the University, but felt himself handicapped in his competition with fellow-students who could give to private study the hours in which he chafed at the dull lessons at the Training College.

Before long he resigned his Training College scholarship and gave himself wholly to University study, with a view to being trained for the ministry. That became possible through the self-denial of his parents and his gaining a small bursary available for those intending to study divinity. He took a good degree and had thereafter a distinguished course at New College. He gained finally a scholarship which permitted him to spend six months in Rome. Rome has many voices and speaks diversely to diverse minds. To Archie the most impressive feature of Rome was the catacombs. The evidence they afford of the conditions of early Christianity fascinated his mind. All other studies were set aside; the catacombs, their inscriptions, their symbols, to these he gave his days and nights. When he returned to Scotland, and as a probationer of the Church preached " on supply " or as a candidate in vacancies, he was never so effective as when he could persuade a minister or a kirk-session to allow him to give a lecture on " The Catacombs of Rome." He never received a " call," but the award of another scholarship allowed him to make a visit to Greece and to the Holy Land. Some time after his return, the gossips of his native village heard with amazement that Archie had " gone over " to the English Church. As his home was almost in sight of Rullion Green, Archie's change seemed to the village folk almost an allying of himself with Dalziel and Clavers and the other persecutors.

I was then in my first year at the University and, when I chanced to meet Archie, and he told me of his decision, I said with the arrogance of youth: " It's not much of an adventure to enter the Church of England." I had been reading Anthony Trollope's clerical novels, which give an impression of the clergy of the Church of England as enjoying fat livings and being much at their ease in their Zion.

I heard later that Archie had been ordained in the Church of England and had done duty as a curate in some English parish. Later still it was reported that Archie was acting as one of the junior clergy of the English Church in Berlin. There he had given his lecture on "The Catacombs of Rome" to the English colony, and the Kaiser had been in the audience. All the quidnuncs said: "Archie is getting on. I wadna wonder if he'll rise as high as that fellow Lang that gaed owre to the English Kirk some years syne."

Then there was no word of Archie for a long time. What Stevenson calls the romance of destiny had meanwhile sent me into England. When I was visiting a Girls' School in Richmond-on-Thames, whose Head was also from Scotland, she said to me: "A clergyman came to my school last month to borrow a map of Palestine to illustrate a lecture he was giving on the Holy Land. His accent was Scottish and I said to him: 'What's your part of Scotland?' When he answered 'Midlothian,' I said, 'Do you by any chance know Mr Stewart Robertson?' 'I should think I do; I used to teach him,'" replied Archie, for it was he, still a curate. I had thought he would have been at least an Archdeacon by that time. He was in Richmond doing temporary duty for an invalid, and as the Head had given the map and received it back, and not thought of asking about his address, I had no opportunity of tracing Archie further.

Some years after, as I was passing through the lounge of a London hotel, a page came up and said: "There's a clergyman, sir, on the other side of the lounge who wishes to speak to you." I followed the page and found Archie, the eyes still bright, the hair no longer as the raven's wing. He talked much of a service which he had just attended for the inauguration in St Paul's Cathedral of the Chapel of the Order of St Michael and St George. He was, as is the way of Scotsmen, rather critical of the officiating clergy's ignoring of the letter *r* in its proper place and insertion of the same letter in an improper place. "Do you remember," he asked, "that you said to me that entering the Church of England was not much of an adventure?" I could only reply: "My sins and faults of youth, why should you not forget?" "Is Miss So-and-so still teaching?" he asked next. "Yes," I answered. "I am surprised," said Archie, "for she's no' a scone o' yesterday's baking."

We parted, agreeing to arrange further meetings. Two months after, when visiting one of my Church of England schools, one of the teachers asked me if I knew Kennington (a district of South London). "All I know of Kennington," said I, " is that some Jacobites were cruelly hanged there after the Forty-Five, that Feargus O'Connor gathered the Chartists on its Common and that the Oval is there." "I went to church in Kennington, last Sunday," said the teacher, "and when talking to one of the curates, after the service, I learned that he knew you: he is the Reverend Archibald Waterston. I have a friend who lives in that parish; she says he works very hard among the poor, and everyone likes him, though they call him the Scotch Curate. He is a great scholar and gives lectures on the Holy Land and the Catacombs of P   ie."

That was in the month in which t   War broke out. Its turmoil and my return to cotland after the War prevented my hearing more of Archie until I heard the comments on the notice of his death this year.

"He hasna made muckle o't." How prone we are in Scotland to assess a life by its worldly success, "unmindful of the crown that Virtue gives . . . to her true servants."

From Buchan to Bologna ‿   ‿

IN spite of Shakespeare's warning, some men
will persist in gilding refined gold and painting
the lily. Such was Thomas Dempster, who, in his
Historia Ecclesiastica Gentis Scotorum, enlarged beyond
all credence the record of famous Scots. Scot and
skill begin with the same letter, and capacity and
Caledonia are initialled alike; whence it is clear
that all men of merit were born in Scotland. By
some such suasive and subtle sorites Dempster
claimed as sons and glories of Albyn the Venerable
Bede, "for he lived much with pious brethren at
Melrose," St Boniface, who converted the Germans,
and seems to have scamped his task, and Boadicea!
Though Cowper did not know it, Dempster knew
that the British warrior queen, whom he called
Bundevica, was daughter of the King of Scots, and
wrote a treatise on "The Besieging of Cities." Occasionally Dempster may admit ignorance, as when
he writes of Romualdus, "who he was or where he
lived, or in what rank of life I have not discovered,
but it is certain that he was a Scot." More often he
invents writers and cites mythical books with a
parade of accuracy and a plenitude of reference
that are vastly entertaining. Who would not wish
to read *The Deeds of Arthur among the Scots*, by Samuel
Beulanius, or *De Albanorum Fortunis*, by Merlin,
"whom the English claim groundlessly as their
countryman," or the book of Duncan MacGruder
of Dunblane on *Poetical Astrology*, or the pamphlet
of William Guild from Aberdeen on *Balaam's Ass*?
Dempster was a child of the ages of faith: he

believed that Guinevere (Gonora) is buried in
Strathmore at Meigle, and that her tomb had
thaumaturgic powers, "quæcumque mulieres locum
calcant sterilescant," that Evenus the Third, the
sixteenth king of Scots from Fergus—look for him
in the Gallery of the Kings at Holyrood and judge
if the charge seems likely!—decreed " ut tot uxores
vir duceret quot commode alere posset," that
Joannes Campusbellus, "vernacule Cammel," was
professor at Bologna in 1260, before that great
University was founded, that there are trees by the
Scottish coast from which fruit drops into the waves
and becomes sea-birds—tammy-norries probably—
that St Mirren, who ruled for many years " Pais-
letum cœnobium," wrote *Homilies on the Saints*, that
St Triduana when pursued by the amorous Nechtan,
whose name abideth in Dunnichen until this day,
tore out her eyes to discourage his advances. Is
not her well still oozing, hard by the kirk of
Restalrig, and misnamed a chapter-house in many
a record, and does not David Lyndsay tell of the
pilgrims who went " to Sanct Tred well to mend
thare eine "? One wonders that man's lust for the
incredible should invent to-day angels at Mons,
Russians at Crewe, and vocal lodges in the vast
wilderness of death, when there are already so
many more marvellous tales garnered in sheaves for
the credulous from the fields of the past.

Dempster knew not truth from myth nor fact
from fancy, unless when writing of his own contemporaries, the many Scots who, as soldiers, students,
scholars, swarmed on the Continent before and
after the Union of the Crowns. His style may be
illustrated by a translation of his account of his
meeting in London with James Halkerston, a brave
Scots soldier and scholar, some of whose poems are
included in *Deliciæ Poetarum Scotorum*. " In the year
of grace 1615, I encountered Halkerston in London

hard by the palace of the great Wolsey, and called him by his name, wondering much at his haggard look and threadbare cloak. Turning to me he said, ' What ill fate brings you here to this land which regards not worth or learning? "Fuge crudeles terras, fuge littus avarum!"' Yet he walked with me unto that Exchange wherein the merchants gather. There, as it was now noon, I besought his company at some ordinary. 'Nay!' said he, ' I have sworn an oath that I shall sit at no man's feast in this relentless city; do you rather be trencher mate with me.' He led me by a grimy alley into a wretched chamber, where he proffered me a broken chair, and seated himself on a tottering bed. To my amazed look of inquiry, he gave answer, ' Yes, this is the shelter ordained for my old age and my gray hair.' From a cupboard he brought forth a coarse loaf and an onion, saying, ' This is what I must offer to a friend for whom the best were worthy, for this is all I have. On such fare I maintain what of life yet awaits me, yet such a spare meal is sweeter than a banquet gained by the arts of the flatterer.' I learned next year that this brave soldier and scholar had perished from want of bread. Let him who reads this story honour the memory of a man of parts and valour, and marvel how little these evil times have regard to bravery and worth."

If Dempster had written his own life with such detail we should have had a scholarly *Gil Blas* or a Renaissance *Jean Christophe* that might have been one of the great books of the world. He includes his own name in his list of Scottish writers, but gives himself the last place on the list "ut meritis et eruditione ultimus est, ita ultimum locum sortietur." Those who have forgotten what a fine language Latin is for narrative might read Dempster in the original and contrast him with Livy and the Cæsar of *The Gallic War*, as he tells some of the incidents of his wandering life. His autobiographical fragment would have needed one of the Tudor translators, or a Lithgow or Sir Thomas Urquhart, to transfer its racy flavour into an English version. Here is its substance, without its tang.

Thomas Dempster was born in 1579 at Cliftbog, in Banffshire, being the twenty-fourth child of twenty-nine whom his mother, Jane Leslie, bore to his father, "baron de Muresk, Auchterless et Killesmont, Banfiae et Buquhaniæ proregem." The Dempsters were noble, especially on the spindle side, but not wealthy, and feuds "cum Curreriis Grantisque" made Thomas's life arduous at its threshold. He learned the rudiments at Turiff from Andrew Ogston "plagosus," but was transferred later to the care of Thomas Carnegie in Aberdeen. Thomas Dempster, senior, in spite of the twenty-nine children, had a *liaison* with Isabel Gordon of Achavachie, who wearied of the auld laird and drew to her the love of his eldest son, men said by sorcery, and persuaded him to marry her. The jilted father disinherited the supplanter son, who retaliated by gathering a swarm of Gordons and assailing his father as he rode with some retainers "ad res provinciæ ordinandas." Several were slain on both sides, Gordons, Sinclairs, Leslies, Ogilvies, and their "famulitii," while the lovelorn father had seven bullets in his thigh and his head split open with a claymore. "Hoc tam inaudito parricidio irritatus" the father sold his estate to the Earl of Erroll, who took the lands but never paid the purchase-money. Justice against the High Constable was hopeless in Buchan, but even its halting foot overtook the elder brother. He had taken refuge in the Orkneys, where he burned the Bishop's palace, and lived "per vim et libidinem," until the isles were too hot to hold him. Thereafter he returned to Buchan with Isabel Gordon and their seven children. He may have been only "handfasted" to Isabel, for he wedded another wife, and, to avoid Isabel's wrath and that of the Gordons, he fled to the Low Countries, that shelter for all criminals, as Dempster names them. The vengeance of God overtook him at Utrecht, where he was torn to pieces by four horses for having treacherously slain his colonel. Thus did he suffer a late and deferred penalty for his crime against God, Nature, the law of justice, and the whole world. Such was family history in Strathbogie in the sixteenth century.

Meanwhile, Thomas junior left Scotland, and became a student at Pembroke College, Cambridge. Catholic Scots were not very welcome at Cambridge, and Dempster before long crossed the narrow seas to France. It was the depth of winter, the Spaniards were besieging Calais, he was robbed of his money, and stripped of his clothes, but the charity and kind tendance of a brother Scot at Montreuil enabled him to reach Paris, and enrol himself in his appropriate nation of the greatest of universities. Plague broke out in the Quartier Latin, and brought Dempster almost to the barque of Charon. When convalescent he set out for Louvain, and found favour with William Crichton, Rector of the Scots College there. Crichton was a Jesuit, and was required by the Black Pope to send some young men of promise to Rome. He selected Thomas Dempster, Patrick Anderson, Robert Hill, who became Professor at Montpellier, and Thomas Lyon, "blind from his cradle." Their sufferings on the journey through Germany were beyond belief. The plague was raging, towns were deserted, the highways and woods were infested with robbers. After more dangers than Othello can have told to Desdemona, or than Ulysses escaped, they reached Rome and found a patron in Cardinal Cajetan, "Scotiæ protectorem," who placed them in a seminary. But the plague, too, had crossed the Alps, and they had to flee from Rome. Dempster, with Andrew Crichton as fellow-traveller, made his way to Tournai, and thence to Douai. There James Cheyne, of the family of Arnage by Ellon, was Rector of the Scots College, and "juventutem Thomæ Dempsteri honestis monitis ad virtutem capessendam accendit," so that he won many prizes and graduated. "Cum tenuis fortunæ ibi spes fulgeret," Dempster left Douai for Paris, and in his seventeenth year began to teach in the College of Navarre. The Scot abroad had the gangin' fit, and Dempster wandered to Saint-Maixent, Toulouse, Nismes, Marseilles, victorious in academic disputations, as vehement for his religious dogmas as for his canons of literary excellence, finding strong friends, and making bitter enemies everywhere. He renounced a high post at Marseilles "desiderio patriæ," and returning to Scotland tried to gather up some fragments of the ancestral property. He ascribes his failure to William Cooper, "or Sathanas," with whom he had publicly disputed on the articles of the Catholic faith at Perth. So poor a stand did Cooper make for the Calvinistic heresy that even the Protestants hissed him. So Dempster bears witness, but it may be said of Dempster, "A' his eggs have aye twa yolks." Once more he left Scotland and returned to Paris, where he taught for seven years, till the flogging of one of his pupils in humiliating nudity raised the byke of the student's courtier relatives against him, and he had to take refuge in England. James VI. and I. welcomed him, as he welcomed all scholars, and talked of religion and Scotland, and the laws of verse, till the envious began to compare Dempster to Robert Carr. The Bishop of Bath was specially enraged that a Catholic should be thus high in favour, and Dempster had to set out on his travels again. He had married in England,

and his wife was so beautiful that men trod each other underfoot on the streets of Paris to see her pass. What a husband says about his wife is not evidence, but there was always a certain liveliness when Mrs Dempster appeared. Perhaps that was why husband and wife went on to Rome, where their daughter was born, and had for sponsors at the font a future pope and an archduchess of Austria. Alas! on the eighth day " parentibus orbis desiderium relinquens cœlum occupavit." It was in Rome as elsewhere; men did not admire Dempster's talents enough, and they admired his wife too much. His enemies, and her admirers, accused him of being a spy, and he was sent as prisoner " ad Turrim nonam." Very soon, however, " superavit invidiam," and found an appreciative patron in the Archduke of Tuscany at Florence. There he wrote *Etruria Regalis*, a mammoth among books, the kind of descriptive work which only a syndicate of scholars would attempt in modern days. It was reissued in a splendid edition in the early eighteenth century by one of the Cokes of the Leicester family. I saw a copy of this later edition in the window of a London bookseller this summer, and a Gordon Highlander looking at it. He had also been at Tournai, and perhaps knew Strathbogie as well as Dempster. The juxtaposition seemed to me a subject for the poets of the north, or for any moralizer who can use the speech of *The Ewie wi' the Crookit Horn*.

Dempster went from Florence to teach at Pisa, and thence to Bologna, where vile men said he was " parum Catholicus," and that he had heretical books in his library. The implication, that a man is to be judged by the books he keeps, rather alarms those of us who may have on our shelves Casanova's *Memoirs* or Salomon Reinach's *Orpheus*, without approving the profligacy of the one or the contentions of the other. But Dempster had nothing to fear. He set off at once to Rome, and by his eloquence, and the Aberdonian excellence of his Latin, convinced the Pope of the baselessness of all the charges of his foes. Alas! his worst foe was of his own household, and less responsive than the Holy Father to rhetoric. Dempster's wife fled from him as Helen from Menelaus, and her Paris was one of his own students. Dempster could have made an anthology from the poets of all ages of passages which describe such faithlessness and the emotions it arouses or inflames. He had probably also explained to his students many a time the accidence of Virgil's line, " Varium et mutabile semper est femina." But as George Eliot says, " Axioms are not axioms until they are proven upon our pulses," and no quotation can assuage desertion or quell the pangs of jealous rage. " Execrabili uxori nequitia concussus " Dempster pursued the fugitive to Vicenza—did he recall the line of Horace?— " Heu, heu quantus eques, quantus adest viris sudor! "—and learned that the lovers had crossed the Alps. The indomitable spirit was broken at last: Dempster returned to Bologna, and died shortly after. He was only in his forty-seventh year, but more than fifty works in Latin are ascribed to him. They graved upon his tomb:

LUGETE BONI, LUGETE DOCTI

Thomas Dempsterus inclytus ille vester hic conditur, ubi Historiam, Poesim, Astræam, Literas, satius condi fuerat. Scotia gloriose genuit, Italia provide rapuit, Felsina pie tumulavit. Æthere Spiritus, hoc lapide Cinis, scriptis Ingenium, ubique Gloria eminet, colitur.

Dempster surpassed most men in strength of body as in powers of mind. He was of great height and a kingly carriage of body, with a huge head, brownish black hair and complexion not dissimilar. In strength and bravery no soldier excelled him, as often in combat he had shown. An unwearied reader, he would spend fourteen hours a day among his books. His memory was such that he may be said not to have known what it is to forget. He would quote from any Greek or Latin writers passages of such length that men called him "the talking library." He could dictate Greek or Latin verses on any proposed subject more quickly than a swift writer could set them down. His style was copious yet rugged: he was rough in manner, the frankest of men, incapable of dissimulation in love or in hate; to his friends ever pleasant and yielding, to his foes fierce and intractable; savagely resentful of an injury and inappeasable against his enemies, yet lacking not the virtues which mark the man who strives after Christian piety. Such is the witness of Matthaeus Teregrinus. That passionate spirit of the Renaissance which Marlowe shows in Tamburlaine, which throbbed in the frail body of Mary Stewart, which impelled on such different pathways the martyr Etienne Dolet and the conqueror Hernando Cortés, may be traced also in the life of the wandering Scot who sleeps beside St Dominic in Bologna.

Whyte of St George's ∽ ∽

SCOTLAND is still the best country to die in.
The Scot cannot see clearly through his tears,
and he will listen to nothing but eulogy as he
looks at the empty chair, still more at the empty
pulpit. Dr Barbour's book on Dr Whyte is full of
matter of interest to Dr Whyte's contemporaries,
but, like most ecclesiastical biographers, he has
mummified his hero instead of making him live.
His book will look very well on the shelves beside
Hanna's *Chalmers*, Wilson's *Candlish*, and Carnegie
Simpson's *Rainy*, stuff out of which someone some
day may make a book on Scottish religious life.
Unless to their contemporaries all these books are
as dry as the remainder biscuit, and destitute of any
sense of values. I lent *Rainy* to a French critic, who
returned it with the comment that surely Scotland
was not so " provincial " as that book suggested.
The word annoyed me, and I asked him what he
meant by " provincial." " Applying terms that
befit the great to the merely interesting, and mis-
taking the local for the universal," was his reply.
I was still annoyed, but recalled that there is
nothing that wounds more sharply than the truth.
Even those of us who love the Free Church feel that
it has always been somewhat of a mutual admiration society, whose verdicts are not accepted *urbi
et orbi*. Many laudators have said in their haste
that Dr Whyte was a great preacher. Is there in
all his sermons anything like the sweep of Chalmers'
eloquence, as an eagle dallying with the breeze, or
like the exploratory thought of Canon Liddon, or

the lucidity and solacing power of Robertson of Brighton, or does Dr Whyte in any degree recall the powers of appeal or the splendour of reasoning of the great French masters of the pulpit, a Massillon, a Bourdaloue, a Bossuet?

Others have said, also too festinately, that Dr Whyte owed his power to his interest in literature. Most ministers travel little in the realms of Apollo. As " in the country of the blind the one-eyed man is king," Whyte seemed a great bookman, although his reading was always under certain restraints. To be learned in literature is no obligation on a minister. He will rarely be taught there how to resolve the mysteries of life or to justify the ways of God. He will not gain from any wide familiarity with the sonnet or the epic any added power to control the lusts of men or to assuage their sorrows. Dr Whyte was a ceaseless reader, but he averted his gaze from more than half of human life as it appears in modern books. All the wide region of physical and natural science, all the vast area of economic controversies, all the movements of philosophical and psychological thought, which have made the last fifty years unequalled in significance since the time of Plato, Dr Whyte passed by on the other side. For these and all such he was out of tune. He read no French, which is to enter into the life of the modern world maimed. If he gave any thought to all that has been written on primitive origins, from Seignobos to *The Golden Bough*, or if he studied what has been taught concerning churches and priesthoods from Kuenen to Loisy, he esteemed it as a tinkling cymbal. He could not have argued for his faith against M. Clemenceau or Herr Pfleiderer. Renan would have loved him and talked with him about Madame Guyon but not about the Song of Solomon. Dr Whyte accepted his beliefs like any contadina who kneels to a wayside

c

Madonna as she climbs up to San Gimignano. He knew in what he had believed, his own inner light, that is independent of creed and country and time. But subjectivities have no power of objective proof. When Dr Whyte was in his early days in St George's, Robert Louis Stevenson, than whom none was more true to the Christian spirit, was wrangling with his father who condemned him as no Christian because he doubted the Church's creeds and their accretions. To Robert Louis Stevenson, and to the world of youth like him, Dr Whyte could not speak. Nor did he speak to their fathers and bid them clear their eyes and discern the weightier matters of the law. Dr Whyte had no historic sense: he interprets Achan as if he dwelt in Heriot Row. He could as little answer the reasonings of Huxley as William Law could meet the arguments of Mandeville. But he knew, like William Law, in Whom he had believed. That gave him great power with believers, but not with Louis Stevenson or the other young men who were declaring with Matthew Arnold " no man can save his brother's soul or pay his brother's debt."

Things are as they are, and biography should present men as they are. Dr Whyte had two great excellences, the one acquired, the other the gift of nature. He had the fullest knowledge of the literature of experimental religion, and he had a wondrous intuition of the movements of the human heart. He knew each chord, its various tone, each spring, its various bias. What a coadjutor he would have made with Molina and Molinos and other Jesuit explorers of the human heart. What a rival he might have been, if he had but had the sense of style of those French moralists, Vauvenargues and La Rochefoucauld, who saw man's nature steadily and saw it feeble as he. A preacher thus equipped is born for higher things than mere eloquence. He becomes a spiritual director, a preacher who reasons, not of fixed fate, free will, foreknowledge absolute, but of personal duty, of individual practice, who sets the secret sins of his hearers in the light of God's countenance.

Burns in *The Holy Fair* describes the sermons of Dr Smith, the forbear of Louis Stevenson, as " cauld harangues on practice and on morals." Dr Whyte's subjects were as those of Dr Smith, yet while at Mauchline " aff the godly pour in thrangs," the eager listeners crowded to St George's. Dr Barbour affords no explanation of this, nor even calls attention to the somewhat consoling fact that man's beliefs are as mortal as himself upon the earth. That string of the human spirit which we call " evangelicalism," which was so diversely caused and so variously revealed in the eighteenth century, brought its own contribution of value to human progress, although it did not grasp this scheme of things as entirely as Wesley and MacCheyne believed. A century before, M. Bergson and Mr William James had realized the insufficiency of reason, and had set in being a pragmatist philosophy without knowing in the least what it had done. The days of evangelicalism were long in the land and mainly beneficent, but age claws all in its clutch, and even the weariest river winds somewhere to the sea. Bad philosophies when they die are said to go to Oxford. Good philosophies, when they grow old and dotage is near, live on in Scotland, and are matter for sermons and stuff for University lectures. The last great prophet of evangelicalism was Robert Murray MacCheyne, whose *Memoir and Remains* is the book most frequent in Scots households after the Bible and Burns, and most abundant on the bookstalls. His name will not be found in any history of Scottish thought, yet for more than half-a-century he influenced as none other the emotions and desires which are the springs of action of the best of his countrymen. He toiled in the slums of Dundee, which are to-day most foul, and in his day must have been unspeakably vile. He pilgrimaged over Scotland to incite seasons of blessing. He journeyed romantically to Palestine, and wrote verses by the Lake of Galilee, and he died in his thirtieth year. He was a most lovable character, more like the figures in the writings of the French mystics of Port Royal or in *The Little Flowers of Saint Francis* than like the ordinary Scottish minister.

In MacCheyne's preachings, meditations, letters, you will find no trace of the urgent philanthropy, the activities in social assistance and reform, the preoccupations with public ethical effort which fill the works and days of modern clergymen. The evangelicals did not leave the Word of God to serve tables of temperance, settlements, housing reform, and guilds. There is a better world they said, but, like the songster of the age, they thought the better land was beyond the clouds and beyond the tomb, and they rather distrusted any urgent effort to anticipate it here. The aids to higher life are all within, they seem to have said, even in the slums and when hours of labour were unlimited. MacCheyne died before the Disruption, but his spirit " came out " in '43, and for a generation and more prevailed in the Free Church. Who that is over fifty years of age in Scotland but recalls the MacCheyne characteristics in thought, tone and gesture of his followers? How strange were their afflatus and their rhythms, their wrestlings, and their groanings that could be uttered only with contortions of the visage, and all the other quaintnesses which could not make the good men ridiculous, for their personal saintliness was always evident, but which did make them incomprehensible to the young. All Scots quinquagenarians recall their sermons, compacted of phrases from which the life had shrivelled, as the mollusc departs from its shell, of misty terms that hid anything definite from the mind, of impassioned appeals to an acceptance that was never suggested as specific acts, and to a belief that was never defined as any scheme of intellection or as constraining to any external activities. As with the schoolmen, universals were the only reals. Man, not men, was all in all. Sin, as something generic, the rebellion of a vassal, the breach of a covenant, was discussed in every degree of tenuity. But sins, the foul deeds done in their days of nature by the men and women in the pews, were never mentioned. Men and women in the Bible record were studied, not as having organs, dimensions, as the people of to-day; they lived under a different " dispensation." That great fundamental checked any sympathy that might well up in the natural heart for King Saul, and too often dashed any hope of help in him who groaned under this body of death.

There was no open vision and no open speech about the temptations of life and the misdeeds of men. Illegitimacy might increase in the Presbytery of Strathbogie, but the crown rights of the Redeemer and the validity of the covenant of grace had never been tampered with in Buchan. Edinburgh, the great citadel of reticence and general ideas, to which Dugald Stewart and Lord Jeffrey had taught the manœuvring of terms as the substitute for thought, and a logical exposition as valid against a sensation, heard from fifty pulpits this rattling of peas in a bladder. In all this valley of dry bones Free St George's had been as the central vale. Conceive, then, the astonishment, the dismay, the interest, the vital thrill, when the young Mr Whyte began to preach morality, when he explored the human heart, when he called his hearers sinners, naming their sins, the covetousness of the merchants, the arrogance of the advocates, the duplicity of W.S.'s, the lasciviousness of the well-bred youths, the malice and uncharitableness of the decorous dames of crescent and square. The wheel had come full circle, but the new Moderatism was more successful than the old. Throngs poured in to hear a minister speak as a spiritual director, a preacher who summoned men to a confessional by his insight into their natures and his detection of their sins, who made the men and women of the Bible stretch out their hands for sympathy through the centuries and speak words of brotherhood—the brotherhood of effort, of failure, of sorrow, and of a short-lived joy—to men and women of to-day who have to face, as they had done, the same dispensation of life.

That was the work of Dr Whyte in St George's, and that is the Scotland I see in the last fifty years. There is little of either on the sandhills of detail Dr Barbour has swept together. We have all a false idea of fixity as strength, and we shrink from acknowledging the mutations which mean life. When will there come a scholar and a saint, a Scottish Sabatier, to trace the sequences of Scottish religious experience and to remind us how variously the bush that is yet unconsumed has flickered and glowed?

A Moray Loon   ❧   ❧   ❧

I LIKE to introduce William of Orange to a class by way of the scoffing rhyme of the Jacobites:

> *O what's the rhyme to porringer?*
> *O what's the rhyme to porringer?*
> *King James he had a daughter fair*
> *And he married her to an Oranger.*

Then I make a pause of surprise that a prince who came from Holland and is commonly known as Dutch William should have been styled Prince of Orange. That leads to wondering where Orange is. If Christmas is near, and the class knows any French, I set them guessing this charade. " My first is a precious metal. My second is a heavenly being. My whole is a fruit, or a town in France." Then we look for Orange on the map of France, and find it in the Rhone Valley north of Avignon. The class gazetteer tells us that Orange was the capital of a small principality, independent under its own counts in the Middle Ages, later coming under rule of the House of Orange-Nassau, and so identified with the history of Holland, and incorporated in France only in 1713. The gazetteer also informs us that Orange is in the Department of Vaucluse and that there is a town of the same name. A boy interjects that Petrarch lived at Vaucluse, a fact which had remained in his memory because the class was studying *The Prologue to the Canterbury Tales*, and the teacher in sketching Chaucer's life had told of Chaucer's meeting with the great Petrarch, who had told him the Clerkes Tale of the patient Griselda. The teacher probably thinks within himself that the Queen of William of Orange was also a patient Griselda, since at her husband's bidding she aided in dethroning her father. He does not impart this adult wisdom to the class. Nor does he think it necessary at this stage to give account of Petrarch's passion for Laura or of the famous sonnets which set a literary fashion, and a mode of amorous exaggeration, for centuries. For Afton Water really rises in the fountain of Vaucluse and not on any Scots moorland.

Can we, however, link Scotland more directly with this region of Roman theatres and triumphal arches, of great churches and literary associations? Let us go a few miles from Orange to another town with a triumphal arch, to Carpentras—nasalize the second syllable and sound the final s—and let us look at its fine cathedral. Near by is the bishop's palace where dwelt in 1535 its most famous bishop, Cardinal Sadolet, in whose life we may find a link with Scotland. Let him tell the story as he set it down in a letter to his nephew Paul. Only I shall turn into English the easy-running Latin of that fortunate time when the tongue of Rome was the common speech of scholars and made a league of nations among the learned. " I was in my library rather late in the evening and was engrossed with some books when my chamberlain came to say that someone wished to speak with me. ' Who is it? ' said I. ' He wears a scholar's gown,' my chamberlain replied. ' Show him in,' said I. A young man entered. Turning to him, but keeping my book in my hand as a hint to him not to linger, I asked what he wished from me. He replied so modestly and with such propriety of language that I laid aside my book and gave him my full attention. ' What education have you had? What brings you to this region? And from what country do you come? ' His answer was, ' I am a Scot.'

' What,' said I, ' do you come from that country
on the very edge of the world? Where then have
you studied?' for his Latin was admirable. ' At
first in my own country at the University of Aberdeen and then at Paris,' was the Scot's reply. ' And
what has brought you to Carpentras?' was my
next inquiry. ' To have the honour of seeing your
Eminence, of whose learning and virtues I have
often heard, and because I was told at Avignon
that you are in need of someone *qui juventutem tuam
hanc erudiret.*' "

To make the story short, Cardinal Sadolet was
delighted with the young Scot and appointed him
professor of eloquence at Carpentras. The name of
the young Scot was Florentius Volusenus, which
has been usually represented in English as Florence
Wilson. He was born " *parentibus ingenuis in
Moraviæ provincia, ad Lossæum amnem amœnis-
simum, haud procul ab Elgino oppido.*" But the name
he bore as a Lossie loon is as little known as the
name of Achilles among the women.

There are few pleasanter towns in Scotland than
Elgin, dignified, serene, whispering from its cathedral
the enchantments of the Middle Ages, and from
its gardens and green spaces the consolations of
nature. When I saw it first, on a golden day in
autumn, it seemed an ideal place for age to wear
away in. " Here," thought I, " a Scottish Cato
Major might be fitly feigned to write a modern
De Senectute. Or here, if Cicero had been a Scot,
would have been his Tusculum, whence he might
have corresponded with Melvin and corrected the
philosophy of Bain. Philosophic disputations could
have no more agreeable environment, suitable alike
to the peripatetics and to those who preferred the
garden of Academe."

Volusenus went from the banks of the Lossie to
study at King's College, Aberdeen, when Hector

Boece was principal of that ancient seat of learning. Boece was born in Dundee, but I leave to others to decide whether the attainments of Volusenus were due to his being a Moray loon, or to his being a student at Aberdeen, or to his being a pupil of Hector Boece of Dundee.

From Aberdeen Volusenus went to London, where we find him tutor to Thomas Wynter, later Dean of Wells, nephew of Cardinal Wolsey.

Another London patron of Volusenus was Antonio Bonvisi, a wealthy merchant born in England of an Italian family from Lucca. Bonvisi, of whom Sir Thomas More said " I was not a guest but a continual nursling of the house of Bonvisi," was the friend of all scholars in his London home of Crosby Hall in Bishopsgate, a mansion with many historical associations. There is a special fitness in the fact that Crosby Hall, displaced from the City, has in our day been re-edified in More's Garden at Chelsea in connection with a hostel for university students.

From London Volusenus went to Paris to study. He held also some position in the household of Cardinal du Bellay, where he may have met the Cardinal's kinsman, the great poet Joachim du Bellay. If they met, I hope Du Bellay read to Volusenus his beautiful sonnet which begins, " *Heureux qui, comme Ulysse, a fait un beau voyage.*" If so, the Scot's eyes would be wistful with memories of the Laigh o' Moray and the Lossie as Du Bellay read, " *Plus me plaist le séjour qu'ont basti mes ayeux Que des palais Romains le front audacieux, Plus que le marbre dur me plaist l'ardoise fine, Plus mon Gaulois Loire que le Tybre Latin.*"

While in Paris, Volusenus acted as a sort of secret agent for Thomas Cromwell, at that time keeper of what Henry VIII. had of a conscience. Several of the Latin letters of Volusenus to

Cromwell are in the Record Office and the British Museum. From Paris Volusenus set out for Rome with Cardinal du Bellay, but fell ill at Avignon, whence he made his way to Carpentras.

It is doubtful if Volusenus was in orders, although he is said to have held an English living. He seems to have been rather the scholar and philosopher than the cleric. He never broke with the Catholic Church, although he had sympathies with the new teaching. It might be more accurate to say that he had, like Erasmus, antipathies against the evils in the Church. Volusenus travelled in France and Italy, but held his post at Carpentras till his premature death, at the age of forty, at Vienne in Dauphiny. "*On revient toujours à ses premiers amours,*" and if Volusenus were not to lie under Moray clods, it was the next best to be buried at Vienne. For Vienne was the chief town of the Allobroges, of whom he had read at King's in *De Bello Gallico*. And at Vienne is a beautiful cathedral, but not more splendid than the fame of Elgin "*templum omnium quæ tum in Scotia erat pulcherrimum,*" as his biographer says. And at Vienne there is a huge "stan'in stane," called "l'Aiguille," but not more impressive than Sueno's stone at Forres, at which Volusenus had gazed with boyish wonder.

The story of Volusenus is that of many known and unknown Scots who in ancient days bore their knowledge for sale and their brains for hire everywhere throughout Europe, the more united Europe, before the schism in the Church and the development of the vernaculars broke the comity of scholars. The names of most of these wanderers are with "*les neiges d'antan.*" But Volusenus has not wholly died, for his book, *De Animi Tranquillitate*, first published at Lyons, "apud Seb. Gryphium," has been several times reprinted. The edition I have was published at Edinburgh in 1751 and

edited by Dr John Ward, who, from Gresham
College in London, dedicated the edition to the
Principal of the University of Edinburgh, William
Wishart, *secundus*, since two of that name have held
that high office.

The book is a dialogue in Latin, taken part in
by Volusenus, Francis Michaelis, and Demetrius
Caravalla. These young men are in Lyons and,
wearied of study, they climb the height of Four-
vières, the Forum Vetus of Trajan, which rises four
hundred feet above the Saône as it rushes to its
union with the Rhone.

The dialogue by Volusenus was without doubt
suggested by the famous *De Consolatione Philosophiæ*
of Boëthius. Volusenus gives it an effective opening.
As the young men are climbing the steep path,
Francis says, "You look downcast, my dear
Florence." To him Volusenus replies, "How can
I but look sorrowful when I know that an English
army is ravaging my native country? Many
Englishmen have been kind to me, and I admire
their king *sed nihil patria dulcius*. And if I try to forget
the woes of my nation, how can I not be moved by
the dissensions about religion when I hear of those
who oppose the pre-eminence of the Roman pontiff
and the dogmas of the Church '*non minore successu
quam studio*'?"

These are the discontents present in the young
man's mind, and so the lists are set for an intellectual
tourney on the best means to secure "*tranquillitas*."
There is elaborate argumentation; there is much
enunciation of wisdom, original and derived, the
ball of argument is tossed backward and forward
very skilfully by all the three: the Latin runs
trippingly from their tongues, that pleasant Latin
of the time, well-girt yet not rigid, lacking something Roman, no doubt; never gold, one must
admit, yet a very pleasing silver. But, but, but,

the man of untranquil mind will come out at the same door as in he went. For many waters of philosophy, be they as clear as the summer Lossie and as full and rapid as the Saône, cannot quench untranquillity. Nor can Scot or Italian or Frank minister to a mind ill at ease by words, words, nothing but words.

As a sample of the style of Volusenus, here is a passage in which he employs a metaphor not unlike that of Tennyson when he likens man seeking for knowledge to an infant crying in the night. "*Puer matrem clam se domo egressam sequitur, sed cum ventum est ad trivium, atque illa nusquam apparet, jam animi dubius et consilii inops, se ad clamorem at lacrymas convertit: nunc huc, nunc illuc, iratus et ejulans, furiosa et incerta erratione se proripit ut inveniat.*"

George Buchanan knew Volusenus well, and wrote a Latin epigram on his death, and cherished the book which the Lossie loon had given as gift to him, the Lennox lad. That gift, a Hebrew Dictionary, is now in the library of the University of Edinburgh.

Willie Laidlaw's Scott ✧ ✧

WILLIE LAIDLAW was grieve to Sir Walter
Scott and author of the song *Lucy's Flitting*.
Lockhart tells us that Scott and Laidlaw and he
were "lounging on the brow of Eildon where it
overhangs Melrose" and talking of the excitement
with which Paris had received *Quentin Durward*.
Scott said: "I think I could make better play still
with something German." Laidlaw broke in: "Na,
na, sir; take my word for it, you are always best
when your foot is on your native heath, and I have
often thought that if you were to write a novel and
lay the scene here in the very year you were writing
it, you would exceed yourself."

I borrow my comment and say: "A Daniel
come to judgment! yea, a Daniel!"

Scott was undoubtedly a great master of romance.
He could bring up the figures of the past as the
Witch of Endor brought up the prophet Samuel.
Dumas, Victor Hugo, G. P. R. James, R. L.
Stevenson, and a horde of others but followed in
his train. But none of Scott's romances of the past,
none of his tales of the days of chivalry, have the
vital reality which marks his novels that are laid
in the times of his father and himself. When his
foot was on his native heath, Scott fashioned characters as real as himself, characters who have
become veritable inhabitants of Scotland. The great
Scott is Scott the realist, who surpasses Scott the
romanticist, however wonderful be his gramarye
in evocation of the past.

All romances date: they have their day and

cease to be. Who knows even the names of the Scudéry romances which the seventeenth century admired and which Scott made the light reading of Edith Bellenden? I tried the other day to read Chateaubriand's *Les Martyrs*, a romance of the early days of Christianity, which was universally admired about a century ago. Not even the sweeping billows of its style could carry me through all its chapters. I might as well have tried to re-read *The Scottish Chiefs* or *The Last Days of Pompeii*. Scott's romances, *Ivanhoe, Kenilworth, The Pirate, Quentin Durward, The Fair Maid of Perth, The Talisman*, are far beyond these. What would youth have been without them, what would age be without the memory of their power? But it is in the novels of the eighteenth century, *The Heart of Midlothian, The Antiquary, Redgauntlet, Guy Mannering. St Ronan's Well*, that Scott shows his knowledge of the human heart, his comprehension of the springs of action, his sympathy with men's sorrows, his understanding of men's joys.

The nearer Scott drew to the eighteenth century the more successful was his art. *Old Mortality* is a great historical novel. The death of Mucklewrath is like a painting by Rembrandt and the denunciation of Claverhouse is one of the rare splendours of Scott's prose. But the Covenanters and Claverhouse have alike the exaggerated chiaroscuro of Rembrandt. These characters were not mirrored from nature as were Cuddie Headrigg, Jenny Dennison, Ailie Wilson. Scott knew people like these; he might have met them any day in a daunder from Abbotsford to Darnick. He never knew a Claverhouse: no one ever knew a Kettledrummle. Scott made his " bloody Clavers " out of books, and there is more ink in him than blood. He smells of the lamp, while Cuddie Headrigg smells of the stable and the byre.

Some have said that Scott "wanted art," as was also said of Shakespeare. Consider with how few touches he reveals in *Old Mortality* Bessie Maclure, or how lifelike in *Guy Mannering* is the mother of Jock Jabos, though we only hear her from behind a closed door, replying to Colonel Mannering as he inquires the way to Kippletringan. Consider the art in that kit-cat masterpiece, Nanty Ewart, in *Redgauntlet*. Would that Scott had written in full the story of Nanty, the minister's son that gaed wrang! Then we might have had a full picture of that wonderful Edinburgh, the hot-bed of genius, at which Scott glanced in *Guy Mannering*.

There is great art in many of his romantic figures. Rebecca in *Ivanhoe*, singing the hymn, " When Israel of the Lord beloved out of the land of bondage came," is a picture as if painted by Ary Scheffer. But it has not the inevitable quality of the scene in which Jeanie Deans meets her sister in the Tolbooth of Edinburgh. How great was the genius, how fine was the art, which could make Jeanie Deans its most convincing figure, its noblest heroine, though, as the Duke of Argyll said, she " did not get beyond a comely sonsy lass." One loves Rebecca the Jewess, though one doubts if she ever really trod the streets of York. Jeanie Deans treads the same earth as Sir Walter did: she has seen the sun set ahint the Corstorphine hills; she is as familiar with the making of cheese and the milking of kye as with self-sacrifice and fidelity to truth.

Scott's contemporaries did not realize his true power. In their reaction against the Revolution they idealized the Middle Ages, and they encouraged Scott to write *pastiches* like *Count Robert of Paris*, *Anne of Geierstein*, etc., instead of keeping his foot on his native heath and near his own time. Some of the novels are, of course, independent of time, such as *The Bride of Lammermoor* and *The Highland*

Widow. These great achievements have the power of a drama by Euripides. Their presentation of hearts riven by tragic fates does not depend on antiquarian trappings.

A sharp contrasting of Scott's romances with his eighteenth-century novels does not mean that one wishes the romances away. Who could wish *Ivanhoe* unwritten? Who has not been thrilled by the siege of Torquilstone and felt his heart leap as Rebecca, watching the Black Knight, exclaims: " He blenches not! he blenches not! " But for the sober certainty of waking life, for the low, sad music of humanity, we must turn to Scott's novels of Scottish scenes, his presentation of Scottish character, the harvest his genius had drawn from the times in which his youth was nourished. Such scenes, such characters, ever held the heart of him who thought of Prince Charlie in Rome rather than of Popes or Cæsars, and who yearned for the view from Bemersyde when Italian landscapes glittered before his failing eyes. For the heart aye's

> *The part aye*
> *That maks us richt or wrang,*

even in the writing of fiction.

Does any historical novel resist the challenge of time? Critics are loud in praise of Thackeray's *Esmond*, but readers prefer *Vanity Fair*. George Eliot wrote *Romola*, a book full of beauty and wisdom. But most of us would give it up for another *Silas Marner*. Flaubert, that worshipper of accuracy, truth, and *le mot juste*, wrote *Salammbo*, a tale of the life of ancient Carthage. Ilk ane maun roose the ford as he finds it, but I have never been able to get through *Salammbo*.

Can a dweller in a present, show dwellers in a past as they were in that past? Or is his vision affected by the intervening centuries as light is

D

refracted when it passes through varying media? Shakespeare's *Macbeth* is a marvellous representation of souls wrecked by ambition and tortured by remorse. Do Macbeth and his wife murder and repent as dwellers in ancient Alban would have murdered or repented? There are in both of them traits of characters, features of conscience, which developed in the ages between the reign of Duncan and Shakespeare's reading of Holinshed. Carlyle declared that the characters in the Waverley Novels were "mechanical cases, deceptively painted automatons." The charge may be true of Galeotto the astrologer, of Henbane Dwining, of Locksley, of Sir Henry Lee, of Berengaria, and other romantic figures. It is not true of any of the figures in the eighteenth-century novels or of many of the figures in the romantic novels, such as those masterpieces of psychology, Conacher in *The Fair Maid of Perth*, Dryfesdale the steward in *The Abbot*, Macbriar the martyr in *Old Mortality*, all of whom are worthy of Shakespeare.

All that Scott wrote gives me pleasure, all except the *Life of Napoleon*. But I discriminate in my love. *The Talisman* was the first of Scott's novels I read. I have a tenderness still for Kenneth, King Richard and Saladin, but I do not place them where I place Reuben Butler, the dominie-depute, or Mrs Saddletree, or Saunders Mucklebackit, or Davie Deans, or fifty others who are as real to me as if they "sat next us in the kirk." You may see in the Clachan of Aberfoyle the coulter which Bailie Nicol Jarvie used as a weapon in the fight in Jean MacAlpine's change-house. I do not smile at the absurdity of showing the real weapon of a fictitious person. Bailie Nicol Jarvie, of whom I know only by reading, is much more real to me than some Clydeside M.P.'s, of whom also I know only by reading.

Robert Louis Stevenson, comparing the romances of Scott with those of Dumas, expresses the opinion that Scott was "surpassed in his own spirit" by Dumas. The opinion would not be widely ratified to-day even in France. Dumas' romances are in literature what the paintings of Delacroix and Delaroche are in art. Neither are transcriptions of the life of France such as one may see in the paintings of Chardin and Millet.

I think that Stevenson himself erred when he took the high road of romance instead of the low road of realism. Only Alan Breck steps out of the canvas in the Stevensonian Hall of Romance. He himself admits to "tushery" in such a tale as *The Black Arrow*.

When Stevenson began to write about Edinburgh lawyers and the folk about the Pentlands whom his youth and his father's youth had known, his wings bore him to things unattempted yet, and he fashioned living women in the Kirstie Elliots of *Weir of Hermiston*.

Sir Walter was the Wizard of the North. But the flares of the magician weaken in the sunlight. It was when Scott looked in his heart and wrote of the Scotland he knew and loved that he mined the gold which Scotsmen will treasure while Tweed runs by Melrose.

A Scottish Spy   ∽   ∽   ∽

FIDELITY may with good warrant be claimed as a Scottish virtue. Loyalty to a cause and devotion to a person may be illustrated from many a page of Scottish history. The gibe of English Cavaliers,

> Traitor Scot
> Sold his king for a groat,

most unfairly misrepresents the transfer of King Charles I. from the Scottish Covenanters to the English Roundheads. Yet as the cleanest corn that e'er was dicht may ha'e some piles o' cauf in't, we need not take it amiss that there is a longish list of Scots traitors who, I hope, are now in Malebolge with Sinon and Ganelon. Our Scots deacon of the craft of betrayal is undoubtedly " the fause Menteith." His odium endureth, and it is still dangerous to " birl the bannock " in the presence of one of that name. Admirers of Montrose raise MacLeod of Assynt to a bad eminence in treachery; Covenanters execrate the lang lad of the Nethertown that helped to take Argyll; and Jacobites and many others count Murray of Broughton as one of the worst of renegades. Sir Walter Scott's father, who was a staunch Presbyterian, and shared in no degree his son's interest in the bleezin stories o' the Hielandmen, threw out of his window the cup from which Murray of Broughton had drunk lest anyone under his roof should put lip to what had been sullied by that traitor. Many of us remember the thrill of dismay

52

which was stirred by Andrew Lang's identification of Pickle the Spy with Glengarry. Some still feel that if the vile truth be as Lang contended he might have been better employed than in playing the sniggering part of Ham. Macaulay has put in his pillory Ferguson the Plotter, a native of Garioch, who became vicar of pleasant Godmersham, in Kent, and was ejected thence at the Restoration. Thereafter he was a sharer in every plot against the Stewart kings until the Revolution, and in every plot for the Stewart kings after the Revolution. Ferguson seems to have had a nature fit for treasons, stratagems and plots, and conspiracy was his vocation. As some Borderers are said to have stolen the beeves that made their broth from Scotland and from England both, so in the troublous times of the Reformation not a few Scots took English bribes while in the service of Scotland, and did their best to serve God and Mammon. Ogilvie of Pourie was a secret agent of King James VI., busy with espionage and propaganda in his sovereign's interest in Italy, France and the Netherlands, yet at the same time in the pay of Queen Elizabeth, a weaver of webs and subterfuges such as scarce any research can fully redd up. I think that Pourie knew himself as a traitor, false to both his employers, and one can only say about him what Bailie Nicol Jarvie quoted from his father, that " the penny siller slays mair souls than the sword does bodies." More interesting is the traitor who, like Macbeth, cannot look upon what he has done, who must so cozen his own judgment as to justify if not his treason at least his purposes. Man cannot endure to see himself as ithers see him, if they see him with scorn. He must drape his misdeeds decorously to his own gaze, and will compass heaven and earth to acquit himself to himself. Stevenson presents such a character in James More, the father of Catriona. George

Eliot has made two marvellous studies of the deceiver who assoilzies himself in Tito Melema in *Romola* and in Bulstrode in *Middlemarch*. It would need her psychological insight to present John Ker of Kersland, who played the part of spy and secret agent and double-dealer in the reign of Queen Anne.

Ker was born a Crawfurd, of the ancient house of Crawfurdland, near Kilmarnock, in 1673, and married a daughter of Ker of Kersland. He bought Kersland from his sister-in-law, and assumed the style of Ker of Kersland. He is as punctilious as a grandee of Spain about his designation, and is Ker of Kersland with all the assurance of a Sieur de Coucy. Ker has recorded his activities and their justification in his *Memoirs*, which were published in 1726 by Edmund Curll, who had to stand in the pillory as a consequence. In the dedication to Sir Robert Walpole, Ker writes: " I have no pretensions to Perfection, but I declare it is the Height of my Ambition to be sensible when I depart from my Duty and to make all the Acknowledgment I can." A commendatory letter prefixed to the *Memoirs* with the signature " Philalethes " was probably written by Ker himself. It contains an ell of genealogy, and declares of Ker that " Corruption and bribery seems in no way to have been his foible."

The Crawfurds and the Kers had been faithful Presbyterians throughout the killing time, and Ker makes a survey of the history of Scotland from the Restoration to the Revolution with a record of the sufferings of his family. When Presbyterianism was re-established in Scotland in 1688 the second temple was not like the first. Many complained that the Revolution Settlement had been false to the lofty ideals of the National Covenant. The ultra-logical of these, our Scottish non-jurors, known commonly as Cameronians, and in Galloway as MacMillanites, refused to acknowledge the Revolution Government or the Established Church. They were true die-hards; they continued their field-preachings, and maintained their military organization. Ker was held in high esteem among the Cameronians while at the same time he was in some mysterious way associated with the plans of the Scottish Jacobites. In the intrigues and disputes which the proposed Union of the Parliaments caused, Ker was an important figure behind the scenes conferring with the Duke of Hamilton, the Duke of Queensberry, the Squadrone Volante, ceaselessly and obscurely. It is hardly possible to realize to-day the passionate opposition which was felt in all quarters in Scotland against the Articles of Union. The Cameronians feared the Union would be a prelude to the restoration of Prelacy and of the evil days of Lauderdale. The moderate Presbyterians doubted if any sanctions could secure their Church against High Church machinations in the united Parliament. Their fears were not without reason. Shortly after the Union the Patronage Act was passed against Scottish protests, and the Church of Scotland was afflicted with a running sore, from which signs of recovery are only now being shown. The Jacobites saw in the Union only a scheme to secure the Hanoverian succession. The Cameronians took strong action: they burned the Articles of Union at the Cross of Dumfries, and they prepared to march on Edinburgh to "raise the Parliament." The Jacobite leaders schemed to bring down the plaided clans in an "entente" with the Cameronians. Ker's influence was high with both, while he had credit also with the Union Party as having been the means of preventing the taking of Edinburgh Castle. The Duke of Queensberry, leader of the Union Party, sent for Ker and sought to engage him in check-mating Highlanders and Westland Whigs alike. Ker talked big: "to dye for my Country or

Religion carried Honour, but to deceive any Man or Party would bring with it a Stigma upon my Name." Queensberry bade him "go home and sleep a night upon it," and finally Ker agreed to become Mr Facing-Both-Ways. There is a long story of intrigue and double-dealing, but in the end Ker addressed the Cameronians at a great gathering at Sanquhar, and persuaded them in an eloquent speech, with citations and illustrations from the Scriptures, "to wait God's own time to deliver us from the Union." The Cameronians returned to their muirs, the Highlanders abode in their glens, the Act of Union was passed; there was an end of an auld sang, and Ker went off to London to claim his reward from Godolphin. Ill shearers get aye bad heuks, and traitors are often betrayed. Ker complains bitterly of how he was treated by "such as I had sacrificed every Thing for that ought to be dear to a Gentleman."

The rest of Ker's life was spent fishing in the drumly water of English politics after the Treaty of Utrecht. The Whigs employed him but suspected him, and even said he "was become a Creature of the Earl of Oxford (Harley)." In 1713 he went on a secret embassy to Vienna to assert to the Emperor that "the honest party," the Hanoverians, was yet strong in England. At Vienna he met as Imperial Secretary the great philosopher Leibniz with whom he ingratiated himself. I have no doubt they discussed philosophical problems. The discussions which Ker had had with Cameronian commentators, sweir to gree, were no bad preparation for debate upon Leibniz's theory of monads. When Ker left Vienna, Leibniz entrusted him with a letter to the wife of the son of the Elector of Hanover, afterwards Queen Caroline. Then and later Caroline found in correspondence with Leibniz some consolation for her treatment by her coarse and disagreeable husband. Ker was at Hanover when the great news came of the death of Queen Anne. Ker had a good conceit of himself and was never backward in proffering or magnifying his services. He reminds me of Andrew Fairservice, and of some Scots in real life, as he recounts with satisfaction how he advised George I. regarding the English people and the best way to rule them and to secure the Hanoverian interest. He came across with the German lairdie, and assures us that all the mistakes of George I.'s Government were due to their not following his counsels. Mar's rising might easily have been prevented if the Ministers had but taken Ker's advice. As they did not do so, " not wishing to be a Spectator of the Miseries my own Country must suffer," he withdrew to Holland. At Rotterdam after " the Fifteen " he met many exiled Jacobites, among them Robertson of Struan, escaped from his cave in Rannoch. Ker describes Struan as " a Man considerable among the Highlanders, and a Man of excellent good Sense, and a compleat Gentleman." I wonder what the Chief of Clan Donnachaidh thought or said of Ker. Struan had a scrupulous sense of honour and a tongue as rough as ready, as his poems show.

After this, Ker flits to and fro between the Continent and England, spying or intriguing for or against the East India Company, the South Sea Company, and the threatened invasion of Scotland in the interest of King James by King Charles of Sweden. His last years were shadowed and unfriended; he incurred heavy debts. He who is bought must buy heavily; and at last Ker was cast into the debtors' prison at the Marshalsea, where he died in 1726. On the last page of his *Memoirs* he makes this moan, " I have seen too much of the Villainy and Vanity of this World to be longer in love with it, and I am myself perfectly weary of it."

He was buried in St George's Church, near the prison. The Marshalsea is gone except a fragment of an ogee wall that confined the debtors, but many Americans visit St George's Church to see the font from which Little Dorrit was christened.

When I visited the church, I recalled rather the lad who was born in Cunningham, who had wandered thus far from Scotland, but further still from the stern simplicities of his Cameronian youth.

Old Parochials ◦ ◦ ◦

EDUCATION in Scotland has been for over three hundred years an affair of the Parish, formerly under Kirk-Sessions, latterly under School Boards. Now that the old order is about to change, it may be of interest to see how the system fulfilled its tasks, so far as Presbytery or Kirk-Session records can show. For success and quiet duty have often no written memorial any more than the due coming of harvest, while failure and " the short corn " usurp pages of record.

There are three Lintons in Scotland, East Linton by the Tyne, the haunt of artists, Linton on the Borders, the home of the laithly Worme which the Laird of Lariston slew, and West Linton on the Lyne Water in Peeblesshire. It is a pity the pleasant Tweeddale townlet has lost its early and euphonious name of Linton Roderick which made it familiar with forgotten years. For Roderick, or Rhydderch Hael, the Christian King of Strathclyde, overthrew at Arderydd in 573 A.D. the pagan forces of Vortigern. You may trace his name, with the help of Sir John Rhys, on the stone by Yarrow Kirk which Sir Walter Scott misread as commemorating the combat of *The Dowie Dens o' Yarrow*. It tells of sorrow much more ancient, for it records the grief of Roderick at the death of his two sons, if conjecture be right in reading its inscription as " hic jacent in tumulo duo filii Liberalis." Our concern for the moment is not with those old unhappy far-off things, but with the schoolmasters of West Linton since the Reformation, and their simple annals.

1602. "The Parish would concur with the minister for sustentation of a schoolmaster, seeing the minister himself is willing to hold hand to the instruction of youth." 1652. On the visitation of the Parish by the Presbytery "the minister reported well of his elders, only stating that he desired that care should be had of the schoolmaster's maintenance." 1658. "Stent-maisters were chosen to break a stent for the schoolmaster, his stipend being ane hundred merks, usual money of Scotland." 1659. "The elders convened, and after prayer nothing of importance coming before them except the agreeing with James Giffard, portioner of Lyntoun, for the buying of his house for a school." 1660. "Mr Andrew Hamilton, expectant, who has resided for two years at Lyntoun as schoolmaster and precentor and has been licensed to preach throughout the Presbytery, having gone into Biggar Presbytery, is to get a testimonial, the Presbytery hearing nothing but good of him." One regrets that the accurate word "expectant" for a candidate has been lost.

When Episcopacy was established in 1669, Lintoun and its minister would have nothing to do with black prelacy. There were still Presbyteries and there was no prayer-book, as Dr MacCrie proved in his severe review of *Old Mortality*. Yet the minister refused to attend Presbytery because Presbytery had acknowledged bishops, whereupon Presbytery styled him "a withdrawing brother." He held to his benefice and his kirk; he was an Elliot, one of "the dour bauld Elliots of auld" of whom R. L. Stevenson sang, and he was still minister at the time of Bothwell Brig and "deposed elders out of his session for going out with the King's Host." The schoolmaster was equally tenacious and impavid. In 1668 it is declared that "Mr James Low, precentor and schoolmaster at Lyntoun, shall officiate no more until he get his license from the Archbishop." Yet in 1688 " Mr James Low, schoolmaster, was one of those who had not taken the Test."

The minister was at last ejected, but his flock adhered to him, and few attended the parish church to hear the " intruded " preacher. In 1688, in the " rabbling of the curates," the intruder was dispossessed, and bauld Elliot entered his pulpit again. The schoolmaster had also been ejected, and had probably kept a scholastic conventicle in some barn between Garvald and Macbiehill. There is plenty of evidence as to the character of the " curates "; the elder Dumbiedykes' friend, Curate Kilstoup, was a sample, but few historians tell us about the substitutes for the ejected schoolmaster. We may surmise what kind of man took the place of Mr Low from *Lintoun Green*, a poem by Alexander Pennecuik of Newhall, dated 1685. The poem is in Scots in nine cantos and the plainest speech. Its stanza resembles that of *Peblis to the Play*, and its frankness is in the same Scots tradition. It calls a spade a spade, and inserts the adjective every time. Pennecuik's choice of subjects bewrayeth him. He wrote *The Merry Wives of Musleburgh*, on the story of " half-hangit Maggie Dickson," whom Madge Wildfire knew, and *The Presbyterian Pope*, on the disciplinary duties of kirk-sessions. *Lintoun Green* is worth reading—though one risks such consequences of a bad Channel passage as Rupert Brooke described —to learn what Scots poetry owed to Fergusson and Burns. It has a motto from Propertius, " saginatus porcus," and the tone is porcine. The " intruded " schoolmaster of Linton and the schoolmaster of Newlands appear in the poem as enemies, under the names of the Boar and the Ass. They have Rabelaisian mishaps such as halflings guffawed over in *Lothian Tam* and other chapbooks of a century ago. Less offensive and more English is the lament of the Ass over his empty school, and his equally childless home—

> *Within my school's deserted walls*
> *None like myself appear,*
> *Bare benches but attend my calls,*
> *For none there sit to hear,*
> *As when at home it so befalls,*
> *I've equal want of cheer,*
> *There but my wife answers my bawls,*
> *And echo only here*
> *Returns a bray.*

After the Revolution Settlement, Presbyteries licensed schoolmasters. In 1694 the Presbytery of Edinburgh " on behalf of the elders and heritors of Lintoun took trial of two young men, which would be fittest to teach the grammar school of Lintoun . . . in several of the classic authors *ad aperturum libri*, also put several grammatical questions to them through the four parts of grammar, to all which the young men gave tolerable answers. The Presbytery judged that both of them have a capacity for teaching the Latin tongue, but that Mr S. is more ready in it, but supposes the other may have more authority in regard of his age." A truly judicial and cautious deliverance. In 1697, " Mr S., Schoolmaster and Session Clerk, gave untimeous advertisement to the Session of demitting his incumbent charge. They notwithstanding, sympathizing with his weakness of ingratitude, allowed him a subscribed testimonial." Mr Robert T. was his successor, and trouble came with him. Presbytery decided in 1702 that there was *fama clamosa* against the schoolmaster of Lintoun. The charges were that " being boarded in John Haddo's house, Mr Robert was observed to be too homely with John's wife by tigging, sporting, conversing, and keeping too much company with John's wife." Also " on a certain day Thomas Alexander and John Anderson came into John Haddo's shop, where they drank a pint of ale, the said Mr Robert and Isobel being present, and that they forgot to call in John Haddo to take a drink with them, which necessitated the two men to make an apology and to call for a pint that John might drink with them, and that Mr Robert replied, ' What need we fash ourselves with him? He is but a senseless body,' and this was spoken in Isobel's presence, and she made no resentment thereof." Mr Robert was young, John Haddo was old, and Isobel was younger. Was it the later Dumas who said that all a play needed was three persons and a passion? When Mr Robert first halted on John Haddo's doorstep, his guardian angel, or the minister, might have advised him in the language of Erasmus's surly innkeeper " quære aliud hospitium." It was proved also that " Mr Robert and Isobel came walking home from Spittalhaugh in one another's hands." The picture suggests Aucassin and Nicolette rather than kirk-sessions. But worse remained behind. John Haddo died, and Mr Robert married Isobel. Thereon the gossips of Lintoun spoke of poison, and nothing was talked of from Carlops to Slipperfield, and from the Cauldstaneslap to Mountain Cross, but the scandal about the dominie. Presbytery dealt with the matter in that full detail which those grave times with their empty days allowed and loved. His minister " had no more to say but that Mr Robert's usefulness was gone as schoolmaster and Session Clerk, as he frequented the naughtiest and lowest persons of the place." In the end, the Presbytery "find him unworthy to continue schoolmaster, clerk, and precentor of Lintoun." When this sentence was read to Mr Robert, " he said openly in the face of the Presbytery that it was club law." There is matter in this story for a novel after the manner of Lockhart's *Adam Blair*, and for the psychologic skill of any Scots Bourget.

Six months later, three students, candidates for

the vacancy, were examined by a Committee of the Presbytery "in classical authors, music, and arithmetic, and after full trial the Committee chose Mr James M." 1710. "On the application of James Alexander in Whitefield, his son Andrew was appointed a poor scholar, and his quarter's fees to be paid by the Presbytery." 1711. "Meeting of the heritors with the elders to consider the decay of the school. It was found to be due to the master not frequenting the diets of education. He was called in, and urged to use all gentle means for regaining those who have withdrawn." 1716. "The Committee who visited the grammar school of Linton reported that the youth in that school did not fully answer their expectations, but they hoped they would amend, for they were yet but young. The schoolmaster was called in, and this intimated to him, and exhorted to carefulness and diligence in the work and a suitable deportment to his station. The schoolmaster being asked if he had any grievance, replied that there were several private schools in the parish, to the detriment of the public school. . . . The Presbytery consider that there ought not to be any private school to the detriment of the public school within two miles of the town of Linton, and recommends the Session to use all due means to that end." 1716. "Mr Gilchrist, minister of Linton, reported that youths were sent out of the parish to other schools because it was reported that they did not get on so well at the public school." 1729. "Complaint was laid before this meeting by the schoolmaster of Linton that a young woman had taken up a private school in the town at Linton, and had withdrawn one half of his scholars, to the great loss and public prejudice of the public school, and craved that this meeting would interpose their authority, and suppress the said school. Which desire the meeting considered

reasonable, and therefore do prohibit and discharge
the said young woman to teach children any further
in the place to the prejudice of the public school."
1730. "It was represented by several of the heritors
that John Wallace, one of the elders, was under
a legal incapacity for voting in the calling of a
minister, because he had used violent rudeness upon
Mr Thomas Baillie, schoolmaster, on which account
Mr Baillie had been obliged to take out a lawburrows
against him." This strange entry is concerned with
the settlement of a new minister, the patron's
nominee, who was opposed by the majority of the
parishioners. Presbytery supported the parishioners,
but the Synod of Lothian and Tweeddale supported
the patron and sent a commissioner to serve an
edict in the church. But "a considerable number
of women came out of the said town" and took
from the commissioner his copies of the edict,
carried him out to the fields and spoke of throwing
him into the Lyne Water. The patron's nominee
was in the end ordained to Linton, though a troop
of soldiers had to guard the fathers and brethren
from the irate mothers in the Lintonian Israel.
The result was a secession, and the building of a
meeting-house. Before that, Mr Baillie had died;
and the elder who alarmed him had admitted his
offence, pleading the extenuating circumstance that
"he had drink that night." 1731. "Mr William
Tolmie, elected by the heritors schoolmaster of
Lintoun, this day produced his testimonials, one
from the session of Dyke, one from the Presbytery
of Forres and a third from the parish of Kilbride.
A committee of three went out and examined him
in Latin prose and verse and in a theme, in all of
which he acquitted himself to satisfaction. And
the Moderator enjoined him to diligence and faith-
fulness in his office, and he signed the formula."
1739. "Mr Charles B. was chosen schoolmaster,"

E

After twenty years of service, his usefulness was endangered by *fama clamosa*. Linton seems to have been as provocative to schoolmasters as Capua to the soldiers of Hannibal. In 1760 Mr Lancelot Whale was chosen schoolmaster and Session Clerk for the parish of Linton, but after six years' service he became Rector of Kelso Grammar School, where for some time he had Sir Walter Scott as a pupil. Sir Walter describes him as " an excellent classical scholar, a humorist, a worthy man." He had a supreme antipathy to the puns which his very uncommon name gave rise to, insomuch that he made his son spell the name Wale, which only occasioned the young man being nicknamed the Prince of Wales by the military mess to which he belonged. As for Whale, senior, the least allusion to Jonah or the terming him an odd fish, or any similar quibble, was sure to put him beside himself. In point of knowledge and taste he was far too good for the situation he held. James Ballantyne, another Kelso " old boy," is not so kind to his master's memory. " The venerable Master Lancelot, an absent grotesque being, betwixt six and seven feet high, was nevertheless an admirable scholar . . . old Whale bore in many particulars a strong resemblance to Dominie Sampson, though it must be admitted combining more gentlemanly manners with equal classical lore."

The life of a schoolmaster in the sequestered vale of the Lyne could have few satisfactions save in the fruit of his labours. Modern times have given to the teacher amenities and rewards of which his predecessors never dreamed. But the teacher's life, whether spent in bustling towns or in the quiet of pastoral hills, must draw its inspiration from the worth of his service and the significance of his task. It was not otherwise with those forgotten dead who rest from their labours and whose examples impose on our gratitude the duty of an equal effort.

Boswell and Johnson ⟋ ⟋

UNTIL recently I had never read Dr Johnson's *Journey to the Western Islands of Scotland*. I had been familiar since school days with extracts from it and could say by heart the sonorous passage concerning Iona. I had indeed recited it as a prophylactic against sea-sickness as I coasted Mull on a voyage to Icolumkill. But I had never, from pure preference, read any of Dr Johnson's writings. I had read *Rasselas* because the decree of the Education Department had imposed that duty on all the students of my time at a training college. I have often speculated on the reason of that extraordinary selection and have come to the conclusion that My Lords meant to offer incense to the "manes" of Miss Deborah Jenkins, who was almost certainly the last to read *Rasselas* from mere hedonism. I had read also some of Johnson's *Lives of the English Poets*, because I was to be examined on these, and some others because I had to examine other people on those. But I think I should have taken up at any time one of Dr Johnson's works only on the justification which he himself gave for presenting an Arithmetic Book to a young lady on his Highland tour, that it was the only book he had.

For, after all, the Dr Johnson who holds so important a place in English literature and in whom the world is still interested is less the writer than the man, and especially the man revealed in Boswell's *Life*. There is no more companionable book, filled with thought yet ever provocative of more thinking, attractive at any page that is opened, and everywhere affording interest and instruction. I place Boswell's *Journal of a Tour to the Hebrides* as high and, indeed, regard it as an integral part of the *Life*. Probably my often reading of Boswell's *Tour* prevented my reading of Johnson's *Journey*. The Oxford Press has recently issued both in one volume, and has given me the pleasure of reading the former once more and the opportunity of reading the latter.

Two books describing the same scenes and incidents could hardly differ more. They support the Berkeleyan theory that the world is created by the vision of the observer. Johnson narrates his experiences: Boswell makes us share his experiences. We sit at home and listen to Johnson's record. Boswell bears us to the Highlands and the Hebrides and makes us companions and fellow-witnesses of his tour. Johnson was a schoolmaster for a time and, according to Garrick, his pupil, not a successful teacher. Boswell probably shared his father's scorn of a dominie. Yet I scarcely know any writer in English who has the qualifications of " the born teacher " in such a degree as James Boswell. The world has been slow in recognizing Boswell's superb artistry as a portrayer of scenes and character. Macaulay said that the *Life* was a great book because Boswell had a small mind. That is mere paradox. Results and causes are not so disproportioned. It was a great power that enabled Boswell to give his convincingness of life to his scenes and the talk of his characters. He takes his place with Scott in the Scottish scenes of his novels, and with Knox in his *History of the Reformation* as a great artist-realist. Scott worked in fiction and Knox described scenes *quorum magna pars fuit*, but Boswell's skill was different as his purpose was different. His aim was to reproduce in others the stimulation which a scene, a person-

ality, a thought had effected in himself. Is not that
the aim of the teacher? I sometimes wish our
masters of method would cease grubbing among
subconsciousness and set their students to discriminate the "differentiæ" of the methods of
Johnson and of Boswell. Such a study might reveal
the conditions of effective presentation better than
all the jargoning of Chicago or of Zurich.

To say that Boswell is dramatic while Johnson is
merely descriptive, would carry one so far, yet is
not enough. Johnson records an incident, Boswell
shows it. All is general and unparticularized in
Johnson. All is specific and detailed in Boswell.
When Johnson describes a pleasant valley near
Achnashiel, it might be anywhere in the world. It
is the conventional valley of the pastoral poets, and
the description smacks more of Tempe or Sicilian
vales than of anywhere near Maam-Ratachan.
Contrast and compare Boswell's account of the sail
from Skye to Raasay. We see Dr Johnson high on
the stern like a magnificent Triton; we share his
fretfulness that his spurs should be lost in the Sound
of Sleat; we hear Malcolm MacLeod sing his
Gaelic song and the chorus of the rowers "Tha
tighin fodham Eirigh"; the spray is in our faces
and the breeze lifts the hair. It is a scene, as Boswell
pictures it, to make a reader in the city abandon
responsibility and duty and trek for the road to the
Isles.

It is easier to feel the power than to analyse it.
I seem to come nearest in saying that Johnson
presents surfaces, while Boswell gives solidities. Or,
Boswell has the stereoscopic power which Johnson
lacks. Zoologists tell of a strange mammal of Java
and Borneo, the spectral tarsier, which was one of
the first mammals to become arboreal in habit. It
developed in its new environment advanced powers
of visualization and became thus less dependent on

its power of smell than earlier forms had been. But the tarsier, though it has wonderful eyes, has not yet developed the power of stereoscopic vision, the various intricate adjustments on which that capacity of precise visualization depends not having yet been evolved. Some observers and some writers are like the tarsier. To call Boswell a stereoscopic artist, in contrast with Johnson, at least suggests the quality of the former's power.

Analogies between the arts are not alluring but ambiguous. Yet one cannot but note that the great school of French art of to-day, which derives from Cézanne, sets as its aim the giving to painting the qualities of solidity, body, stereoscopic effect. But let others hunt that hare.

Johnson was, without doubt, a greater man than Boswell in power of thought, in force and depth of character, and in the impressiveness of his life. Johnson's worth was himself, and none of his writings give the full impression of him. To see him in breadth and depth *totum, teres et rotundum* we must go to Boswell's *Life*. Boswell's worth was in his sensibility—in the older sense of that word—of which his account of how he was moved by tales of the Forty-Five is an instance, and in that something defying analysis which makes the artist.

All this does not mean that Johnson's *Journey* is not an interesting, and even a great, book. It is best to read the *Journal* and the *Tour* and thus enjoy the felicity of the patriarch who wedded Rachel *and* Leah. The first feature that strikes the reader is how little Johnsonese there is in Johnson's writing. Occasionally he may make the little fishes like whales but few of his polysyllables cannot be justified by their precision or comprehensiveness. Johnsonese is mainly to be found in Johnsonian imitators, and some of the worst offenders have been Scots. Lord Kames, perhaps, has raised himself to a bad eminence in this respect, but it cannot be denied that Scots schoolmasters have always had a tendency to drive the mammoths of vocabulary. At least I have never heard anyone dare to say " homologate " except a Scots schoolmaster.

For the most part, the style of Johnson's *Journey* is easy, lucid and straightforward, with nothing in its language that is unusual or pedantic. One is conscious of a latinity of structure rather than of language, as in the sentence, " What rent they paid, we were not told, and could not decently inquire." Johnson often uses the passive voice where his contemporaries would have employed the active voice. That is probably also a Latin trait. Modern usage imitates him in this respect, but the preference for the passive is in our time a sign of the tendency to devolve responsibility on the community or on chance. Latinity of structure, however, seldom spoils Johnson's sentences, although it makes the following clumsy and confused. " Among other guests a visit was paid by the Laird and Lady of a small island south of Skye of which the proper name is Muack which signifies ' swine.' "

On many a page of the *Journey* the reader will pause to note one or other of those passages " of high sentence " which Johnson could so admirably frame, and which are our English parallels to the aphorisms of the great French makers of maxims. These are like a judge's summing up : they make one realize what Hobbes meant by " fortresses of thought," and they justify the laudation of Johnson which Boswell transferred from Baker's *Chronicle*— " Scarce ever any concocted his reading into judgment as he did." Johnson's aphorisms sometimes merit the name of epigram since the latter term suggests the flash of wit rather than the resonance of wisdom and an appeal to vivacity rather than to love of truth. Different readers will class as a maxim or as an epigram his comment on the unwillingness of the professors of St Andrews to show him the ruined chapel of St Leonard's College. " Where there is yet shame, there may in time be virtue." All Scots, at least, will class as a mere epigram the following, " A Scotsman must be a sturdy moralist who does not prefer Scotland to truth." It is not true, of course, yet one cannot say there is no truth in it. Nor was Johnson without skill in satirical innuendo. When he says of Glasgow, " The college has not had a sufficient share of the increasing magnificence of the place," he shows he can use a dirk as well as his more usual claymore.

The *Journey* reveals all Johnson's prejudices against Scotland and its Church. Yet he never shuts his eyes to reality that confutes his prejudices, as is shown by the high tribute he pays to the ministers he met in Skye. Many of his prejudices are so clearly the result of ignorance that a Scot nowadays is only amused by them, though the Scots of his own time were enraged.

One cannot but regret, however, that there was no one at St Andrews or at Elgin to set right his absurd error that Scottish reformers destroyed either cathedrals or abbeys. Cathedrals and abbeys in Scotland, like abbeys and many churches in England, fell into neglect and then into ruin because the nobles who had obtained the lands, which before the Reformation maintained these churches, devoted all the produce of these lands to their own purposes. I wish there had been a Chesterton to tell Johnson of the Russells " with the plunder of a hundred churches shod." To preserve a cathedral from decay needs hundreds of pounds annually. To keep Westminster Abbey from falling down has meant thousands of pounds in the last ten years. There are as many ruined abbeys in Yorkshire as in all Scotland, but no one at Rievault or Fountains blethers about reforming mobs destroying stone buildings in a few hours.

Not the least interesting passages in the *Journey* are those which tell of little details which travellers often ignore. Johnson was accustomed to the latticed windows of England and found the guillotine windows of Scotland a hindrance to his desire for fresh air. The references to goat's flesh in Highland meals reminds us that the Highlands had not in his time become pasturage for sheep, whom one of their own poets describes as

> *the gray-faced nation*
> *Which swept our hills with desolation.*

Johnson was pleased with his Scottish meals, and that is a very characteristic sentence in matter and manner which refers to Scottish breakfasts: " If an epicure could remove by a wish in search of sensual gratification, wherever he had supped he would breakfast in Scotland."

It is a good test of a book whether we wish it longer. I wish Johnson had made his *Journey* longer and had told us about the men and women of Edinburgh over whom he casts the unrevealing mantle of this fine sentence: " We now returned to Edinburgh, where I passed some days with men of learning whose names want no advancement from my commemoration, or with women of elegance which perhaps disclaims a pedant's praise." That is like giving a man a bill of fare instead of a breakfast, or, as Johnson might have expressed it, affording him the unsatisfying reflection of Barmecide. Fortunately, we have Boswell and his *Tour* to supplement the omissions of the *Journey*.

George Fox in Scotland ⌒ ⌒

I KNEW a Scot exiled in England who counted it a partial compensation for his banishment that he had come to know the Society of Friends whom the world calls Quakers, a term originally of opprobrium, but now significant of purity of purpose and zeal for whatsoever things are noble. Even in England the Quakers are a little flock, but they have had an influence on national ideals and in social reform out of proportion to their numbers. They have been pioneers in many a venture of progress, and in our own time their strength of confident faith is not abated nor their vision of humanity's needs in any whit dimmed.

The Quakers have never had much influence nor any but a tiny following in Scotland. Perhaps the rigidly intellectual form which religion assumed in Scotland after the Reformation afforded less scope for the testimony of the Friends than the sacramentarianism and symbolism of England. Yet if George Fox was the founder of the Society of Friends, Robert Barclay, laird of Urie in The Mearns, was its St Paul, its teacher and reasoner, its philosopher and theologian, its propagandist, whose *Apologie* is only one of many writings.

A soldier's son, of ancient lineage, educated at the Scots College in Paris, Robert Barclay, like William Penn, was one of the few mighty in the world's regard who joined George Fox and endured the obloquy and persecution suffered by the early Quakers. Barclay was wholly without honour in his own country, and the citizens of Aberdeen only jeered when he walked through their streets in sack-cloth and ashes as a testimony against their town, a scene which Whittier has described in an effective poem.

George Fox himself had scarcely more success when he extended his preaching journeys to Scotland. These journeys are recorded in *The Journal of George Fox*, of which a new edition has been recently issued. The book is not so well known as it deserves, and may be commended to various classes of readers, to those who care to study the mysterious ways in which the mind of man moves, to those who delight to read of the days of other years, and to those who take pleasure in simple straightforward English deftly used.

George Eliot tells of a lady who read religious biographies with amazing celerity and zest. When she saw "grace" or "sanctification" on a page, she skipped it. When she saw "rheumatism" or "marriage," or any references to taking medicine or leasing property or disputing with relatives, she read carefully and with enjoyment. Persons of similar temperament may read Fox's *Journal* with interest if they follow her procedure. When they see "I saw a steeple-house and it struck at my life," or "many people were convinced of the truth," let them skip like young lambs. Even if they skip as the kangaroo they will find much matter of a mundane and positive kind. It would, of course, be very much better if they would read all the *Journal*. There are few, perhaps, like Tam Halliday in *Old Mortality*, of whom Jenny Dennison said "he wadna ken that he has a sowl except that he swears by it." But there are many Gallios who care for none of those things on which George Fox was so eager.

George Fox visited Scotland for the first time in 1657, entering by the West Border, and giving

his first address before the Earl of Nithsdale in
Caerlaverock Castle. Few who visit the ruins of
that romantic fortress think of associating it with
the Quakers. But fact has a way of making even
more piquant associations than fiction can devise.
Thence he proceeded to "The Heads" and
"Badcow," places which I do not know under these
names. Fox seems to have been received most
favourably in the West Country and on the Border,
and the only references to Quakerism which I can
trace in Scots literature are placed in the same
regions. Galt in *The Annals of the Parish*, makes the
Reverend Micah Balwhidder recount how two
Quakers, leather-dealers from Kendal on business
in Kyle, invited all who cared to a meeting in
"Friend Thackam's barn." Thackam thought it
necessary to tell everybody, "Na, they're nae freends
o' mine; I hinna ony English relations." But the
minister admitted that when the initiatory silence
was broken, "The Quaker gave a praiseworthy
Gospel discourse."

George Fox, in his Scottish journey, addressed
gatherings at Glasgow, "in the Highlands," at
Stirling, Linlithgow, and in Edinburgh. In the
capital, the priests, as Fox always calls all ordained
ministers, stirred up opposition and he was summoned before the Council and ordered to quit the
kingdom within seven days. I do not know if some
humorous Scot suggested to Fox that he would be
leaving Scotland by going to Fife, but instead of
returning to England he made his way to Burntisland
and thence to "Johnston." Fox, on principle,
would not say St Johnston, and he might have been
pleased, as many of us are not, that the indwellers
of St Johnston have changed that swelling name
to the unimpressive monosyllable, Perth. The folks
of St Johnston would not listen to the Quakers, and
the governor sent a company of foot to eject Fox

and his companions from the town. " We got on our horses, and James Lancaster was moved to sing with a melodious sound in the power of God, and I was moved to proclaim the day of the Lord." Nevertheless, they were boated over to Gowrie, for this was one of the many occasions when Tay had broken the Brig o' Perth. The scene may be commended to some artist in the Fair City as a subject for a picture.

" Being thus thrust out of Johnston we went to another market-town," says Fox. The town was almost certainly Dundee, and the Quakers held a meeting on the market-day. Ian Maclaren misleads the Sassenachs by representing in his novels that Scottish farmers on market-days discuss only sermons, ministers, and the doings of presbyteries. Home-keeping Scots know it to be otherwise, and that the spirit of Martha rather than of Mary rules in marts and markets. Fox and his friends found it so in Dundee, and he laments, " Alexander Parker went and stood upon the market-cross with a Bible in his hand, and declared the truth amongst the soldiers and the market people. But they, being a dark carnal people, gave little heed and took little notice of what was said. After a while I was moved of the Lord to stand up at the Cross and declare with a loud voice the everlasting truth and the day of the Lord that was coming on all sin and wickedness, whereupon the market people all came running. . . ." Truth is advantaged by a Boanerges in Dundee and elsewhere. From Dundee the Quakers went to Leith, and Fox, disregarding the ban of the Council, preached in Edinburgh, made another visit to Perth, and then set off for England by way of Dunbar, where the steeple-house " struck at my life."

He sums up thus on his Scottish tour : " When first I set my horse's feet atop of Scottish ground, I felt the seed of God to sparkle about me like innumerable sparks of fire. Not but that there is abundance of thick cloddy earth of hypocrisy and falseness that is atop, and a briery brambly nature which is to be burnt up with God's word and plowed up with his spiritual plow . . . but the husbandman is to wait with patience."

Patience is still the most necessary equipment of those who labour in Scotland to change our briery brambly nature.

Mrs Somerville ᐁ   ᐁ   ᐁ

THE name Burntisland is an anglicized absurdity, in spelling as in pronunciation. Brunteelan, which is more euphonious and less scornful of its sources, keeps, however, its meaning inscrutable, being as the name of Achilles among the women, a thing of surmise and not of knowledge. Burntisland is a pretty town still as it lies under the sheltering Binn and gazes across the firth to Edinburgh, like some nymph adoring her divinity. A century ago one would have had to go far to find a town of more alluring aspect or more picturesque emplacement. The quaint old church on the promontory dominated the little haven under the hill. On the east the whin-speckled links sloped to a sandy shore, while cliffs and shelving beaches, mantled with verdure, made a bolder romantic scene to the west. The railway, like a too ardent lover, has been the assailer of Burntisland's charms, and has delved its parallels in beauty's brow. When Burntisland became the ferryport of the Forth, displacing Pettycur, the iron road threw a barrage across the links and bade the indwellers become troglodytes before they could reach the sea. When the giant bridge leaped the estuary at Queensferry the steeds of steam burst through the western cliffs, crossed the bay, now incarnadined by aluminium works, and trampled and disfeatured the seaboard path to Aberdour, our Scots equivalent for the enchanted ways by Clovelly and Ilfracombe. Is progress worth its price, and has industrial development brought anything to equal what it has taken away?

79

I see this old Burntisland, the old-world ways of the folk of this little grey town on the windy shore, in the *Recollections* of Mary Somerville, who in the eighties of the eighteenth century played among the whins and the rocks by Starleyburn. There is no romance which fictionists feign that is so strange as the romance of destiny. Who, looking at the little girl digging for " buckies " among the sand, could have foretold for her a European celebrity as a scientist, the renown of a great mathematician, the applause of London, Paris, Rome, and the distinction of giving a name to a women's college at Oxford?

I see this old Burntisland and the old-world days, the daughter of a naval officer who had some cousinred with the Scots peerage, Fairfax of Cameron. Mary was not a native of Burntisland. Her mother went to London to take farewell of her husband, who was setting out for naval service against the American Republic. On her return journey she reached the manse of Jedburgh, the home of her sister, and there her daughter was born. Mary often in later years visited her birthplace, and took great delight in the " Eden scenes by crystal Jed." In the manse she found her second husband, her cousin, by whose name she is known to the world.

Mary's mother was loving and kindly, but somewhat " thraveless "; her father was often away on long cruises, and there was little order in the hoose when the guidman was awa'. Mary ran wild, knowing all the birds by sea and shore, gathering shells and seaweeds on the rocks, learning to read, she hardly knew how, going to the kirk to be catechised and answering the " questions " at the minister's visit, although she " did not understand one word of the Catechism," yet at the age of nine unable to write. She tells how the minister on one occasion asked a servant, " Peggie, what gave light to the world before the sun was made?" Peggie replied, "Deed, sir, the question is mair curious than edifying." Peggie's discriminating comment should be borne in mind by examiners. Of course, Mrs Fairfax had relatives who censured her easy way with Mary. Above all, there was Aunt Janet. The situation reminds one of "the aunts" in *The Mill on the Floss* when they are proving their kinship by finding fault with Maggie Tulliver. Happy are those who have cousins whom they can reckon by the dozens, and a hive of aunts; they will be aware of their shortcomings and be inured to frankness. All of Aunt Janet's self, her views on life, and all the accepted subjection of women are in her comment to Mrs Fairfax, "That lassie, Mary, shews nae mair than if she was gaun to grow up a man!" At last, at her father's instance, Mary was sent to a boarding-school at Musselburgh.

Musselburgh is another Scots town with which time has dealt hardly. Within living memory one might have named it as a haunt of ancient peace and an example of urban charm. Tranquillity brooded over its broad High Street, guarded by the Pinkie gates and dappled with the shadows of its mercat-cross and picturesque Town House. Its high-walled gardens had an unrivalled wealth of plums. Its steep-pitched roofs and frequent dormers had tones and shadows to test the whole range of an artist's palette. You might sit in the umbrageous Mall and, as the scent of tansy drifted to you from the gravelly bed of the devious Esk, might see in fancy every figure of Scottish history for nine centuries caracolling over the arches of "the Roman Bridge." On the links a few Edinburgh lawyers and Lords of Session pursued leisurely the acknowledged game of the senescent, or rested from their labours in "Mrs Forman's." The western window of that hostelry surveyed the mien of those, triumphant or

F

dejected, who had passed, like Dante, through
Pandemonium. Towards the harbour, in the wynds
of Fisherrow, one peeped into kitchens tapestried
with teacups, and might fancy from the binks set
high with delf and the quaint dress of the fish-
wives that one were wandering by the Zuyder Zee.
Alas! Troja fuit: chimneys, mines and mills have
encinctured " the honest toon," and the sons of toil
and grime are noisy in its streets.

The head of Mary's school was Miss Primrose,
and, in spite of her name, she was without understanding of the springtime of life or of young folks'
minds or bodies. Mary Fairfax had to learn by
heart pages of *Johnson's Dictionary*, and " I was
enclosed in stiff stays with a steel busk in front,
while, above my frock, bands drew my shoulders
back till the shoulder-blades met. Then a steel rod,
with a semi-circle which went under the chin, was
clasped to the steel busk in my stays." The girls
played at ball, marbles, and " Scots and English."
This last was a mimic similitude of a raid on the
Debateable Land. " The little ones were always
compelled to be the English, for the elder girls
thought it to be degrading." It is doubtful if Mary
learned much at Musselburgh. Even her easy-
going mother was disturbed to learn that Mary
could write only " in half-text," and that she wrote
to her brother about " a bank-knot." The error in
spelling indicates the Fife pronunciation of " note "
at that time, as of many good Scots folks still.
Mary's education may be said not really to have
begun till, on a visit to Jedburgh, her uncle, Dr
Somerville, told her of the learned women of ancient
and Renaissance days. The kindly minister assured
her that it was not impossible for a girl to learn
Latin, and he offered to read Virgil with her daily
Sympathy and suggestion? Good Dr Somerville
knew their power long before M. Coué. From that

time Mary Fairfax was assiduous in search after knowledge. As she was now growing up, she was sent to Edinburgh to learn dancing, drawing, and generally to be " finished," as the word of the time was. There she first learned of algebra. " When I was visiting a Miss Ogilvie she showed me a monthly magazine with coloured plates of ladies' dresses, charades and puzzles. At the end of a page I read what appeared to be simply an arithmetical question, but on turning the page I was surprised to see strange-looking lines mixed with letters, mostly x's and y's, and asked, ' What's that? ' ' Oh,' said Miss Ogilvie, ' it's a kind of arithmetic: they call it algebra, but I can tell you nothing about it.' " Her drawing-master, Nasmyth, also told her to study Euclid, but this was another mystery. " As for going to a bookseller and asking for a Euclid, the thing was impossible." At last her brother's tutor, Mr Craw, procured her Bonnycastle's *Algebra* and Simpson's *Euclid*, and thenceforward her mathematical studies went forward like a house on fire.

Miss Fairfax, however, never was the mere bluestocking. She enjoyed the society of Edinburgh, played, painted, " did not dislike a mild flirtation," turned readily from surds to eightsome reels, and passed from quadrilles to quaternions with equal zest. The only fault in the delightful Edinburgh society of the first years of the nineteenth century was, according to Mary, the bitterness of political feeling. Mary's family was Tory, her own sympathies were Whig, and even more advanced. Whigs, in the mode of the Revolution, wore their hair short; Tories were faithful to the traditional queue. Mary expressed admiration of the cropped hair of some young advocate, which brought from her father, now Admiral Fairfax, the declaration that a man who cut off his pigtail should have his head cut off also.

In 1804 Mary married her cousin, Samuel Greig, Russian Consul in London, who "had a very low opinion of the capacity of my sex, and had neither knowledge of nor interest in science of any kind." She does not say why she married him, but it is clear that she spent three dull years in London, from which she returned to Burntisland a young widow with two boys. Disappointed in matrimony, Mary turned to mathematics, studied Newton's *Principia*, and made the acquaintance of Professor Wallace, of the University of Edinburgh. He gave her a list of the great French mathematicians—La Grange, Monge, Callet, La Croix, Biot, La Place, etc. " I was thirty-three years of age when I bought this excellent little library. I could hardly believe that I possessed such a treasure when I looked back on the day that I first saw the mysterious word Algebra and the long course of years in which I had persevered almost without hope." Another encourager was Professor Playfair, who had passed from the pulpit of Liff and Benvie to the Chair of Natural Philosophy in Edinburgh. They compared notes with each other on the writings of La Place, the dominant figure of that age in mathematical astronomy, and especially on the *Mécanique Celeste*, then a wonder and still unequalled.

In spite of her grave studies, or by reason of them, Mrs Greig was like Tibbie Fowler—"a' the lads were wooin' at her." "One of the persons who was paying court to me sent me a volume of sermons, with the page ostentatiously turned down on a sermon on the duties of a wife, which were expatiated upon in the most illiberal and narrow-minded language. I thought this as impertinent as it was premature, sent back the book, and refused the proposal." Her cousin, William Somerville, was more successful, and married her in 1812. He seems to have been a man of high attainments,

genial disposition, and lovable nature, but quite
satisfied to be a satellite to the planet he had wedded.
He encouraged her studies, he made summaries
and notes for her, he made calculations for her—
her addition was weak—and he schemed and con-
trived acquaintance with Herschel and Sir Humphry
Davy in London, with Arago, Humboldt, Biot,
Cuvier, La Place in Paris. Here was a husband
worth the having, fit acolyte for a hierophant of
Urania! Mrs Somerville had the gift of description,
and her sketches of persons and scenes in London
of the 1830's are vivid. She was present at the
coronation of George IV., and " while the pageantry
and noise was at its height Queen Caroline demanded
to be admitted. There was a sudden silence and
consternation—it was like the handwriting on the
wall." Up to this time Mrs Somerville had been
content to devote herself to the absorption of
knowledge in mathematics, geology, mineralogy,
astronomy, physics. She had never thought of
being herself either an expounder or a discoverer of
scientific truth. Lord Brougham summoned her
from receptivity to action when he asked her to
translate and explain in English the *Mécanique Celeste*
of La Place. Diffident of her powers, she wished to
decline, but Somerville and Brougham persuaded
her to undertake the work, which was published
under the title of *The Mechanism of the Heavens*. Its
success was immediate, and rewards streamed on
her in a flood. The Astronomical Society made her
an honorary member, the Royal Society resolved
to place a bust of her by Chantrey in their hall, the
great Whewell of Trinity wrote what he thought
was a sonnet in her praise, she was *fêted* at Cambridge, and, these being the days of unmarried
fellows, a four-post bed was set up in the Master's
Lodge at Trinity for her and Somerville. Finally
Sir Robert Peel advised the bestowal of a Civil List

pension of £300. Paris echoed the pæans of England,
and in the brief Second Republic, " The President
invited me to a very brilliant ball he gave, but as it
was on a Sunday I could not accept the invitation."
Was that not a victory for Burntisland over Paris
and a tribute to the power of those impressions of
youth when she had handed her token to the elder
on Sacrament Sunday?

The career of authorship thus auspiciously begun
continued for forty years till, at the age of eighty-six,
Mrs Somerville published *Molecular and Microscopical
Science*. After 1850 she lived mainly in Italy, interested in everything—Popes, Pompeii, votes for
women, spectrum analysis, the eruptions of Vesuvius,
the flowerets on its slopes, the prevention of cruelty
to animals, the voyage of the *Challenger*, the transit
of Venus, Shakespeare, Dante, Darwin, the sorrows
of Paris in the Commune, and the sufferings of the
thrushes at Sorrento, *quicquid homines agunt* and
all they seek to know. She lived to be ninety-two,
and sometimes her thoughts went back to the days
" when I used to scramble over the Binn at Burntisland out after tods-tails and leddies' fingers." The
closing passage of her autobiography is itself a
revelation of the character of this sailor's daughter
and noble Scotswoman. " The Blue Peter has long
been flying at my foremast, and now that I am in
my ninety-second year I must soon expect the signal
for sailing. It is a solemn voyage, but it does not
disturb my tranquillity. Deeply sensible of my
utter unworthiness and profoundly grateful for the
innumerable blessings I have received, I trust in
the infinite mercy of my Almighty Creator." She
died at Naples, 1872, but Scotland phrased that
farewell, and moulded its hopes. " *On revient
toujours à ses premiers amours.*"

Presbyter and King ∽   ∽   ∽

I WRITE of Robert Bruce—not the hero-king, but a Scots minister who opposed a king who was not heroic. " Cuidich an Righ " is the duty of many beyond Clan Kenneth, but to withstand a tyrant-king may sometimes be a patriot's highest service. " Think ye," asked Mary Stewart, facing Knox at Holyrood, " that subjects, having power, may resist their princes? " " If their princes exceed their bound, Madam," replied Knox, " and do against that wherefore they should be obeyed, it is no doubt that they may be resisted, even by power." To stand as firmly before his sovereign as Knox, and to claim as strongly the freeman's right, made the renown, as it made the sufferings, of Robert Bruce of Kinnaird. There are many Kinnairds in Scotland; the cliff which the fisher dreads on the coast of Buchan; the castle of Duthac de Carnegie which the Lindsays burned; the Kinnaird with " the bright burn " which R. L. Stevenson praised; the Kinnaird where Carlyle companied with Charles Buller; the bold peel in Gowrie which " caret vate sacro," though it has the aspect of the dark tower to which Childe Roland came. The Kinnaird of which Robert Bruce was laird lies between the deserted village of Airth and that railway Quatre-Bras where wandering locomotives continually do cry, Larbert in the vale of Carron. There, about 1554, Robert Bruce was born, second son of Sir Alexander Bruce of Airth. He had " a lang pedigree," claiming that the hero who sleeps at Dunfermline was one of his progenitors. Pride of ancestry that leads only to chanting " Fuimus " may enfeeble, but the blood of the Bruce impelled this Robert to be worthy of his sires. Young Robert studied at St Andrews, in France and Flanders, and widened his mind by contemplation of men and cities. His father purposed him for the law, and hoped his son should wear the ermine. But one clear call had come to Robert, and only the ministry of the evangel seemed to him a possible way of life. He wrote to James Melville: " Ere I cast myself again into that torment of conscience which was laid on me for resisting the call of God to the ministry, I would rather go through a fire of brimstone half a mile long." " O ter quaterque beati," those for whom in life's morning the way is thus clear before their footsteps, and who hent each stile merrily, heedless of other trackways and bypath meadows! That is a beatitude rare for modern youth, hesitant, perplexed, drawn hither and thither, veering before the multitude of counsellors, and swithering which pathway it shall tread.

Robert Bruce's most noted ministry was in Edinburgh, and a contemporary account describes it as " most comfortable to the good and baneful to the enemies." In the post-Reformation days in Scotland, pastoral duties were far from being the chief task of a minister. Kings found an unmitred Church raising its head in councils even more proudly than bishops and abbots had been wont to do, Robert Bruce thought it his duty to concern himself with affairs of State, while King James VI. felt sure he needed neither guidance nor aid in ruling Scotland.

Few kings have been more frequently or more ignorantly " written down " than King James VI. Men of letters cannot forgive him his detestation of tobacco; novelists seem aggrieved by his chastity. His unhappy mother and his hapless son are assured

of the undying interest of the world by their tragic
fates. The Sixth James, the only successful Stewart,
the only one of the dynasty who accomplished
" the plan that pleased his boyish thought," has
few partisans, and no admirers since the translators
of the Authorized Version addressed to him their
adulatory dedication. Sir Walter Scott portrays
him " the saftest o' the faimily " in *The Fortunes of
Nigel*, and there are few who seek to read further.
The advocatus diaboli has an easy task in reckoning
the faults of James VI. Historians have been ready
to make him the occasion of epigram and rhetorical
antithesis rather than to call attention to his wide
learning, his diligence, his skill in diplomacy, or
chicane—*l'un vaut bien l'autre*—excelling that even
of Queen Elizabeth, his shrewdness in judging character, his love of peace, and his acute perception of
how to achieve his purposes and beguile or restrain
his adversaries. If James had ruled in the eighteenth
century, Carlyle would have praised him as he
praised Frederick. If James had reigned in our days,
he would have been lauded in Peace Conferences
and praised by Mr Lloyd George and C.O.P.E.C.,
and would have passed his days in a blaze of
eulogy.

James had declared in 1590 that the Church of
Scotland was " the sincerest kirk in all the world."
Yet shortly after he was scheming to establish that
prelatic system which, like a sword that pierces the
hand that holds it, was to destroy the Stewarts.
Robert Bruce was the most steadfast opponent of
all James's direct and indirect efforts to make " that
stubborn kirk " stoop to the yoke of Episcopacy.
Besides opposing the King in his attempts to subvert
Presbyterianism, Bruce rebuked James for his seem-
ing slackness in the punishment of evil. The history
of Scotland records many mysterious murders, but
few of these slayings have made such a sensation as

the murder of the " bonnie Earl o' Murray " at
Donibristle. Everyone even to-day knows:

> *O lang, lang will his lady*
> *Look owre the Castle Doune*
> *Ere she see the Earl o' Moray*
> *Come soundin' thro' the toun.*

James took no steps to bring the murderers to
justice, and Robert Bruce publicly rebuked the
King from the pulpit, " desiring His Majesty to
humble himself before God and confess his negli-
gence." Such outspokenness is not heard to-day,
perhaps because there is no evil in high places to
rebuke, perhaps because modern men are less
intrepid than Robert Bruce. The baffling Gowrie
mystery, which Mr Andrew Lang's explanations
have but further beclouded, raised other reasons of
quarrel between Bruce and his royal parishioner.
At last the outspoken preacher was banished to
France, and, though the time of his exile was short,
Bruce was for the rest of his life " in the wilderness."
King James had by this time gone to rule in
England, that " bieldy bit," as Scott makes him
describe it. Thence he ruled Scotland, as he boasts,
" with ane pen " more surely than all his forbears
had done with the sword. Inverness, Aberdeen, the
Castle of Edinburgh, were assigned, in succession,
as places of restraint for Bruce, but in 1615 he was
permitted to dwell in his own manse of Kinnaird.
So many resorted thither, seeking advice on matters
of doctrine and practice, that King James gave
orders " not to allow any more Popish pilgrimages
to Kinnaird." Bruce was not prohibited from the
pulpit, and he preached at Larbert, where he
built a church, and at Stirling. His sermons
were for long a Scottish religious classic, and
neighboured *The Fourfold State* and *The Christian's
Great Interest* on eighteenth-century shelves. His
contemporary, Livingstone, said of him, " Never

man spoke with greater power since the Apostles' days."

If James VI. chastised Scotland and Robert Bruce with whips, Charles I. chastised both with scorpions. But the harbour was being neared for him who had been, as his friend Calderwood quoted from the *Æneid*, " terris jactatus et undis." Robert Bruce died at Kinnaird in 1631, and was laid in an aisle of the old kirk of Larbert. More than a century after, his descendant, James Bruce, the famous explorer of Abyssinia, was buried near him. The Ancient Nile and the Dark Continent had laid their spell on this later Bruce, who faced their dangers and terrors as dauntlessly as his ancestor had endured the threats and the prisons of a king. As the ages pass the forms of service may change, but the inspiration of duty endureth for ever.

The Writing of Scots

WHEN Sir James Barrie was yet Gavin Ogilvy, before he gave up to fantasy what was meant for reality, those who love the braid auld Scottish tongue took pleasure in the skill with which he presented the speech of his Angus weavers. He did not always remember that " the Scots tongue has an orthography of its own, lacking neither authority nor author." Yet it is a slight thing that he should have spelled " kyowowy" which he explains as " particular," when Jamieson spells " kiowows." The lexicographer explains the word as " things of a trivial nature " and cites Latin *nugæ* as a parallel. A " kiowowy" body is therefore one who has not put away childish things. Unless Thrums has glossed the word to another meaning than prevails elsewhere, Pete Elshiner should have said to Tammas Haggart, " Ye're owre pernickety, Tammas," not " Ye're owre kyowowy."

When Eppie Guthrie's son made a fortune and on his way back to Thrums married at Tilliedrum a lass jist seventeen years auld, Jean M'Qumpha said, " I sepad he's mair ashamed o't in his he'rt than she is." The word " sepad " occurs not in Jamieson nor, indeed, anywhere in print, except in Sir James Barrie's books. Philologists among his readers could make nothing of it at first, and took refuge in declaring it a borrowing from the Gaelic or an invention of the author. Yet " I sepad " was only a writing down of what Gavin had heard, but should have spelled " I'se uphaud," or, at fuller length, " I s'al uphaud," or, in English, " I shall uphold." The phrase sounds like the expression of a firm determination, and recalls that motto of the House of Orange, " Je maintiendrai," which Dutch William enlarged rather adroitly when the Protestant wind brought him to Torbay. " I sall uphaud " was a strong asseveration in early Scots, but, just as " I sall " was worn away to " I'se " and the aspirate ignored, the meaning was also triturated till " I'se uphaud " meant only " I think." Gavin Ogilvy heard the phrase, and set it down as one word.

His error leads one to consider the differences amongst authors who have written Scots verse or prose since English became the accepted speech of Scottish public life. When Robert Burns wrote Scots, he drew from the Scots he spoke daily and heard daily, and from the Scots he read in the song-books in which he delighted, and in the writings of Fergusson, Gilbertfield, Allan Ramsay, and other writers of the generations immediately preceding his own. It cannot be proved that he was acquainted at first hand with Scots literature of its great age, nor does his Scots show forms transferred from Dunbar, Gavin Douglas, Henryson, or David Lyndsay.

Sir Walter Scott heard Scots spoken daily: he could speak Scots as readily as any farmer of Liddesdale or gutterbluid of Edinburgh, such as Green Breeks. He had read in the whole range of Scots literature, highways and byways, from Wyntoun and Sir Tristram to his own day. The Scots of Burns was the Scots he spoke and heard and read. So was the Scots of Sir Walter Scott, although the range of his reading was wider. A threefold cord is not easily broken. The power of these two writers, in their use of Scots, comes from this trinity of experience which they wove into the unity of their art in Scottish prose and verse. Has any important writer of Scots held the same three strands since?

There is no greater master of Scots dialogue than John Galt, in whose works are the best examples in modern times of the pith and smeddum of the ancient speech. But there is little trace in Galt of any influence from previous Scots literature. He wrote Scots as he had spoken and heard it from his youth up, but he did not have the third strand. In Robert Louis Stevenson we have a skilful user of Scots for verse and prose-dialogue, but he also had only two strands, not the same two as Galt had. Stevenson had read widely in Scots literature, and has drawn from its stores phrases, words, rhythms, cadences. He had also heard plenty of Scots spoken, more at Colinton and Swanston and Bridge of Allan and Stobo, of course, than in Heriot Row. Could he speak Scots easily and naturally? He reports John Todd's "drawling Lothian speech" very well, but did he himself speak anything but Edinburgh English to John Todd? Stevenson writes "Lallan, dear to my heart as the peat reek, auld as Tantallon" very skilfully, but was it ever the normal language of his lips, still less of his thoughts? His own witness is " the language spoken about my childhood." He had the two strands, reading and hearing.

Sir James Barrie's Scots shows no trace of influences from previous Scots literature. It is Scots as he has heard it. That explains " sepad," and the error suggests that he does not speak Scots, at least not Angus Scots. If so, he has but one strand. If he has a speaking Scots, it is more likely to be that of the Border, learned in his school days in Dumfries. Probably the Angus speech impressed him the more by its very difference on his return to the town of his birth. The incomer is more gleg than the native to note vivacities or oddities of speech.

Dwellers in Rome are stated to have detected a certain Patavinity in the Latin of Livy, the native of Padua. So Stevenson said that to him, as a man of the East, Burns was sometimes as something foreign. He felt more at home in the " brave metropolitan utterance of Sir Walter." It is noteworthy that he writes " utterance," in which one might without violence read a confession that his eyes and ears were familiar with Scots, but that his lips have not the true facility. It may be doubted if the threefold cord will ever again draw argosies into a Scottish haven. Well! the twofold cord is a strong one also. And I'se uphaud it may yet draw treasures from the deep.

On Speaking Scots ◦　◦　◦

MOST English people and many Scots folk think that "to speak Scots" is to speak an incorrect form of standard English. Much bad Scots is spoken in Scotland, as much bad English is spoken in England. The braid auld Scottish tongue, when spoken or written in the traditional manner, has a stronger claim to be termed "correct" than even standard English, if by "correct" we mean "adhering to the earlier forms."

An English lady once said to me, "I heard a Scottish boy say, 'That's hit' for 'That's it.' Are the Scots careless of the aspirate as some English are?" My reply was, "King Alfred said 'hit,' just as the Scots boy did."

The modern pronoun he, she, it, was in Old English he, heo, hit, but standard English has suppressed the aspirate of the neuter form. The supersession of "heo" by "she" reads like a cinema story. "Heo" deserted her spouse "he," who consoled himself by concubinage with "seo," the Old English feminine demonstrative. It is quite in the tradition of such unions that "seo" should have toshed herself up and become "she." I understand that "heo," degraded to "hoo," may still be heard in Lancashire.

A Scots boy would say "Thae hooses," when an Englishman would say "These houses," and a Cockney "Them 'ouses." The Scots boy pronounces the noun precisely as Harold Hardrada did. He and the Cockney are faithful to primitive use in their demonstratives. They (thae) and them

were originally demonstratives, and did not become
personal pronouns till after Senlac. We have seen
that the feminine of " he " abandoned his company.
His plurals, which were " hi " and " hem," did the
same. Undismayed, he allured " they " and
" them " to act as his plurals. The Scot, imper-
meably conservative, still uses " they " as a demonstrative. What has he to do with Hastings or Duke
William? The Londoner who says, " Let 'em all
come," has not truncated " them." Omission of
" th " is not a Cockney error; he has beheaded the
ancient " hem." He is using still the pronoun which
was familiar to that king whose name was Ethel-
rede, the man of noble counsel, but who, as good
counsel was ever lacking in him, was ekenamed
Un-rede, the man of no counsel. Alas! there
came a day when a maker of school books, who
had not read Burns and knew not the meaning of
" reck the rede," changed the bitter sarcasm into
Ethelred the Unready, which has neither bite nor
relevance.

English has thus lost and gained through the
centuries. So also has its alphabet. The alphabet
of Old English was fortunate in having two characters for the two sounds which we represent by
the one symbol th, as in " thin " and in " thine."
One of these old characters looked like a " y." I have
seen a church bazaar described as Ye Olde Fayre,
the words being set out in Gothic type to increase
the effect of archaism. But he who knows the history
of English pronounces " ye," as " the," not as " ye."
Old Scots documents abound in " ye," " yt " (that),
and similar usages, but he who is a deacon of the
craft of language will always say the words with
the " th " sound.

It is also a false archaism to write " fayre " for
" fair," meaning market, though it would be an
accurate archaism to describe one of the stall-

G

holders as a " fayre ladye." Fair, meaning market, is from French *foire*, from Latin *feriæ*, holidays; there never has been a " y " in the word. Fair, meaning beautiful, is from Old English *faeger*, as in Harold Haarfagr, who was worsted at Largs. The change from " g " to " y " and thence to " i " is frequent in English, as when Old English hlafdig became ladye or lady, with its plural ladies.

Another character of the Old English alphabet has become obsolete. It was like a " g " with the side of the head removed, but many scribes wrote it as " z " with a tail. It represented the sound of " gn " in the French word *gagner*, the central sound in the name Menzies when that is said correctly. It has degenerated to a mere " s " in MacKenzie and Dalziel, but retains its true power in Ben Chonzie, Monzievaird, and that polysyllable from Uam-var, Calzieebohalzie. I am told that Carrick folk ignore the " z " in Colzean, at which I am sorry. All who wish to speak as their forbears did will sound " z " in Scottish names with its original power.

Scots and standard English are both derived from Old English, their relation being like that between Dutch and Deutsch (German). It is an error, however, to think that there was any uniform language throughout England before the invention of printing. Caxton laments the diversity of dialects, and tells an amusing tale of a sailor shipwrecked in Kent, who asked a farmer's wife for " eggys," on which she told him she could not speak French. When he pointed to what he called " eggys," she told him these were " eyer." On which Caxton asks, " What is a man to say—eggys or eyer? "

The many diversities of mediæval dialect could, however, be grouped in three main classes— Southern, Midland, Northern. These are best distinguished by their different forms for the plural of the present tense of verbs. The South said, as in the motto of Winchester School, " Manners makyth man." The Midlands said, as in Chaucer's lines,

> Smale foules maken melodie
> That slepen all the night with open ee.

The Northern dialect, to which Scots may be traced, said, as in Dunbar's line, " Unto the death goes all estates," or, as in Henryson's *Burgess Mouse and Uplandis Mouse*, " For commonlie sic pykers luiffis nocht licht," or, as in Gavin Douglas's praise of spring, " Tidy kye lowis, veillys (calves) by them rinnys." " When the kye comes hame," though written in the nineteenth century, follows the traditional Scots syntax, " When the kye come hame," is bad grammar in Scots.

The Scots relative pronoun " whilk " has wholly fallen out of use, though Byron employs it to get a rhyme. As Saturn was dethroned by Jupiter, whilk has been supplanted by which, a softer form of the same. Old English had no relative pronouns. Languages seldom have such in their early stages. A sense of relativity is late in language and in the mind of man. Old English in the days of Caedmon used as relatives the personal pronouns with what a Greek grammarian would call an enclitic. At a later date the interrogative pronoun " hwa," modern who, was made to do double duty. In the twelfth century another interrogative, " hwile," compounded from hwi (why) and like, was conscripted for relative duty. Southern tongues softened the word to which, Scots held to the stronger form, which they preferred to spell quhilk.

No Scot should need to be told that " quh " is not said like " qu " in queen, but is said as " wh," as in Boquhan, Balquhidder, Loquhariot, and other lovely names. A Scot who speaks of Balquhidder, making the medial syllable " quid, " should be deprived of his tobacco for a year, or should be required to go up Balquhidder on his knees, right from King's House to the head of Loch Voil, and to say ten times at the grave of Rob Roy, "And a better bairnie I will be."

Translation into Scots ✧ ✧

A S a strong mind grasps readily the thoughts of
others, a strong language will have power to
express the content of another speech. Is Scots a
good medium for translation? Scots literature began
with translations. When John Barbour professed
to be writing history he was often translating from
French romances. Henryson of Dunfermline's
Robin and Makyne is a translation, with improve-
ments, from a work of Adam de la Halle of Arras.
The first translation of Virgil's *Æneid* into any
vernacular tongue was Gavin Douglas's version in
Scots. Dr Neilson proved that *The Complaynte of
Scotland* was a translation, with variations, from
Alain Chartier. Of the Renaissance and Reformation
translators into Scots, it may be said as of Gad,
" a troop cometh."

The tradition failed, except for Sir Thomas
Urquhart, when Scots literature weakened after the
Union of the Crowns. Those who ascribe that
decadence to religious causes imagine a vain thing
and are ill read in comparative literature. English
literature sank similarly after the Norman Conquest,
when French and Latin were the accepted tongues
of thought and fancy. As English poetry had its
rebirth in Chaucer, Scottish verse had its renaissance
in Allan Ramsay, whose translations are often
better than his original work.

Horace was Allan's chief quarry. He renders
" Mæcaenas atavis edite regibus " very aptly as:

> *Dalhousie of an auld descent,*
> *My stoup, my chief, my ornament.*

He translates, adequately and Scottishly, " Vides ut alta stet nive candidum " into :

> *Look up to Pentland's towerin' taps,*
> *Buried aneath big wreaths o' snaw.*

He betters his original when he turns " Dissolve frigus, ligna super foco large reponens " into :

> *Then fling on coals and rype the ribs,*
> *And bek the hoose baith but and ben ;*
> *That mutchkin-stoup, it hauds but dribs,*
> *Sae let's get in the tappit-hen.*

" Nil mortalibus arduum est : Cœlum etiam petimus stultitia " is a truly Horatian line. It gains a vernacular ruggedness in Ramsay's translations :

> *What is't man winna ettle at ?*
> *E'en wi' the gods he'll bell the cat.*

Mr J. Logie Robertson, as " Hugh Halliburton," the shepherd of the Ochils, has in our own day devised versions of Horace of equal felicity if less faithful to the letter of Flaccus.

One of the oddest of translations into Scots is the Rev. Dr Hateley Waddell's *The Psalms frae Hebrew intil Scottis*, which was followed by a translation of Isaiah. The title-page of the former bears the Burning Bush, with the motto, " Nec Tamen Consumebatur," translated as, " It lowe't and was nane the waur."

That monosyllabic pithiness recalls to me a translation, made by the Rev. John Struthers, of a motto on a sundial in an Oxford college. The inscription reminds the passer-by that the hours " pereunt et imputantur." A simple translation would run, " The hours pass but you must give account of them." Struthers compressed the warning into, " By, but no' by-wi'."

In the 23rd Psalm Dr Waddell translates, " My cup runneth over " as " My bicker is fu' and skailin." His opening stanza of the 100th Psalm begins,

" Skreigh til the Lord, the hail yirth maun ye." His prose falls often into a regular rhythm and even into rhyme. He renders, " There is a river, the streams whereof make glad the city of our God " as " A river rins wha's wimplin wins to gled the brugh of God."

Professor Alexander Gray, of Aberdeen, has shown how the elusive Heine may be inveigled into breeks and bonnet, and has been very skilful generally in translating German verse into Scots. The most expert of modern translators into Scots was probably the late Professor Mair, of the University of Edinburgh. He quarried mainly in the Greek Anthology, as did Ben Jonson when he wrote *Drink to Me only with thine Eyes*. W. J. Cory made from the same collection a beautiful rendering of the lament of Callimachus for his dead friend, the poet Heraclitus:

> *I wept as I remembered how often you and I*
> *Had tired the sun with talking and sent him down the sky,*
> *And now that you are lying, my dear old Carian guest,*
> *A handful of grey ashes, long, long ago at rest;*
> *Still are thy pleasant voices, thy nightingales awake,*
> *For Death he taketh all away, but these he cannot take.*

An epitaph in the Anthology runs in English prose, " I, Dionysus, lie here, sixty years old, I am of Tarsus, I never married, and I wish my father never had." Professor Mair turns it into Scots rhyme:

> *Here I, Jock Scott, frae Peterheid,*
> *Aged sixty-twa, lie cauld and deid,*
> *A bachelor, for wed I wadna,*
> *And, och ! I wish my faither hadna.*

In Book I. of Martial's epigrams you will read, " Nubere Paula cupit nobis : ego ducere Paulam nolo : anus est : vellem si magis esset anus." Professor Mair's version is:

> *Peg's willin' ; aye, but there's a barrier,*
> *She's far owre auld for me ;*
> *She's thirty-nine, I'd up and marry her*
> *Gin she were ninety-three.*

Alyth ✑   ✑   ✑   ✑   ✑

THE name is said as "aileth." If philology be
ignored, the pronunciation may support the
town's claim to assist convalescence by its bracing
air and salubrious site. Like an old plaid with gay
new fringes, Alyth is spread on the braes which
guard Glenisla and gazes resolutely across Strathmore towards the sun and the Sidlaws. A Ninianic
missioner, Moloch, a sinister name for a preacher
of the Faith, reared its first church on a knoll whence
men might gain the widest view of the strath and
the fullest sight of heaven. A later generation,
under the Roman Obedience, built a small worthy
sanctuary in which varying creeds were proclaimed
and a variant ritual seen for seven centuries. The
old fane was deserted a century ago and a braw
new kirk was built. There remains to-day on the
ancient site only a fragment of a chancel with a
trinity of bold arches on Romanesque pillars. Two
generations ago they echoed to the sound of Psalms,
yet they look as if they had been ruinous since
Malcolm the Maiden.

The church was the hearth of the old town's life,
and the indwellers built their homes near its walls
and enclosing its graveyard. A sleeper in an Alyth
house in the ages of Faith might turn in his bed and
see, through the bole of his chamber, the light
gleaming before the pyx. Then he might turn
again to slumber, assured that the powers of
darkness had no universal sway. Windows still
give on the graveyard, and those who lie under
blankets are but a few feet from those who are happed
more securely under turf.

Alyth has a High Street which is but a wynd and
a civic centre, the Cross, which three converging
carts would block.   Both recall the times when
goods were borne up the glens in creels on shelties.
The Mercat Cross was unwisely removed from its
little carfax to a site in the lowest town, where it
looks " wandered."   It bears the date 1670, the
lion passant gardant gules of the Ogilvies, and the
initials of James, second Earl of Airlie.   He was the
son of the brave lady who wadna come doon from
the Bonnie Hoose at the bidding of the gleyed
Argyll.   Captured at Philiphaugh, he was doomed
to the embraces of " The Maiden," but escaped from
prison disguised in his sister's clothes.

The new town, though drab and touzled at the
railway station, as if putting its worst foot forward,
is yet a pleasant place with an enticing individuality.
To compare small things with great, it resembles
Annecy and Bruges.   A stream runs through its
streets and square as in the Savoy town.   You may
stand on the bridge and see several other bridges,
under which the stream frolics as no Flemish canal
can do.   Like the Shunammite who dwelt among
her own people, Alyth seems a place apart, and the
autochthones distinguish themselves scrupulously
from the incomers.   Yet Alyth had one crowded
hour of life which assured it a place in the history
of Scotland.

When Scotland, united as rarely before or since,
was fighting against Cromwell for Kirk and King,
her first army was broken at Dunbar, her second at
Inverkeithing, her third at Worcester.   Monk was
sieging Dundee while English ships held the Tay
and English gunners the castle of Broughty.   There
was need, therefore, for wisdom and resolution at
Scottish G.H.Q.   Direction had been entrusted to
a committee from the estates and the General
Assembly.   This War Cabinet forgathered at Alyth

that it might be in touch with Middleton, who was planning to bring down the Gordons for the blue banner by Deeside and Glenshee. As the burghers of Alyth scanned the dignitaries who collogued at the Cross or in the kirk, they pointed out the Earl of Crawford, the Earl Marischal, their own Lord Ogilvie, Leslie, Earl of Leven, the hero of Duns Law, and several ministers talkative about strategy. One of these was James Sharp, minister of Crail. No spaewife from Forfar or claimant to the second sight from Rannagulzion would have been believed if forecasting his future.

Dundee was more than twenty miles off; the Isla by Crathie was riding-deep and set about with pools and myres; the direct pass by the Glack of Newtyle was rough and of ill repute. So G.H.Q. at Alyth, lords, lairds, ministers, deeming themselves safe, went to bed. Meanwhile a wide-awake Englishman, Colonel Aldred, with a troop of horse, was galloping from Dundee by Meigle and Balhary. As the morning lightened over Kinpurnie his troopers swept across the Market Muir into the little town and captured the Cabinet of Scotland. An English news-letter of the time says that Leslie was found " hidden in a cupboard." What a humiliation for the soldier who had charged beside the great Gustavus and had checked the onsets of Wallenstein. But the statement is due to the ignorance of the Sassenach regarding Scottish furniture. Leslie was in bed, in a box-bed, not very distinguishable to English eyes from an aumry, a place of reservation.

The captives were sent to Dundee and shipped thence to the Tower of London. As they plashed through the burn of Alyth, what were the thoughts of Sharp of that ilk? It is strange that the burn of Alyth has no name. More denuded than the Red Gregarach, it is nameless, by night and by day. Did some ancient tabu forbid utterance of the name

so that in time it was forgotten as the Jews from
excess of reverence lost the name of Jehovah? Or
was its kelpie a maleficent sprite so that canny folk
kept a wise silence regarding him?

He who follows the burn up to the Den of Alyth
will not credit that it has a dread past. Mediæval
poets liked to make their poems begin on a May
morning, and culled their choicest phrases for
descriptions of the spring. It would task a whole
choir of poets to praise fitly the Den of Alyth in
May-time. Above the burn, crystal in its shallows
and amber in its pools, a brighter flood of verdure,
shimmering in the sunshine, ripples over bank and
cliff, on haugh and scaur. Birch and alder, tasselled
larches, oaks golden in their youth, and emerald
beeches cast their swift shadows on the grass gemmed
with violets and on the glowing clumps of whin.
Here and there the gean is snow-white as a bride
arrayed for her husband.

O foolish James Sharp, to covet lawn sleeves and
a jewelled mitre when you might have seen the
recurring spring outvie the splendours of prelacy
by the burn and braes of Alyth.

Sparrowcroft ✎ ✎ ✎ ✎

IS not that a pleasing name for a street? Yet street is too assuming a term for the row of about a dozen houses in the ancient burgh of Canmore in Angus. You leave its High Street, along which motors rush and gurgle; you pass under a pend into a wynd where forestairs give sharp angles of shadow on the sunny pavement; you mount a stey brae which has a handrail for the assistance of the elderly, and for the safety of all in seasons of frost; you turn a corner, and there, secluded, serene, is Sparrowcroft. A century slips back; you feel the air of Cranford, and you would not be surprised to meet a Scots Miss Matty or Lady Glenmire herself. The thoroughfare is about fifteen feet broad, paved with reddish oval stones, like a mosaic of cookies and kidney potatoes. Each door has a knocker that gleams, and above snowy doorsteps, knockers of gold and thresholds of silver, the windows are swathed, like the heads of nuns, in the white of screens and curtains; the blinds are venetian, with every tape secure. Sparrowcroft looks an ordained dwelling-place for spinsters, quiet precincts in which maiden aunts may practise elegant economy, as they said in Cranford. The houses have a " prunes and prism" aspect, not that they frown, but just as if they were saying " Hush! my dear."

Twice a day a stream of noisy life, however, flows over the cobbles. Sparrowcroft is not the most direct access to the neighbouring school, yet, for some unapparent reason, the pupils make it their favourite avenue to the place of learning. The boys draw a stick along the garden railings to make that noise which is neither a ratatattat nor a rubadubdub, but like a hermaphrodite combines disparate joys. The girls saunter through in pairs or linked trios, all chattering at once. Feminine subjectivity needs no external world to summon its energy, as is the fate of man. A Tennysonian dweller in Sparrow-croft would quote, " There, twice a day the Severn fills." When the tide of juvenility has ebbed Sparrowcroft seems to heave a sigh of relief. So a *grande dame de l'ancien régime*, prisoned in the Conciergerie might breathe more freely when the daily tumbrils had rolled away, assuring her of one day more at least of life. Yet Sparrowcroft enjoys its secret thrill as the younger generation throngs noisily by its doors. Even serenity will gain a savour from an occasional susurration, as men snuggle deeper in their warm beds when the wind whistles along the eaves.

Sparrowcroft houses have gardens which may claim to have, as the hanging gardens of Babylon, no peer or analogue. There would seem to be only three ways of placing a garden in relation to a house. Either the garden is in front of the house or the garden is in rear of the house or the house is islanded in a circumambience of garden. Each arrangement has its own defects. An anterior garden is more in view of passers-by than of the occupants of the house. A posterior garden scorns the passer-by, and has an aspect of selfishness. Its house dwellers must go to it to enjoy its pleasures, for it is rarely visible from a sitting-room window. The peripheral garden escapes these drawbacks. Its penalty is that one cannot survey it with compre-hensive view as Napoleon cast his glance over Elba. It reveals itself but as you move around it. Thus it is symbolic of life, in which also there is always

something unseen round the corner. Such uncertainty does not allay the restless mind with the
anodyne which a perfect garden should afford.

Sparrowcroft has found out a fourth possibility.
Its gardens are on the other side of the thoroughfare
and in full view of the houses. A Sparrowcrofter
may sit by her front window and look across the
cobbles to her own garden railings, her own garden
gate, her own flowers, with " nihil alienum " before
her eyes. She is monarch of all she surveys, her
horizon decked with her own honeysuckle and
roses. She sees a small thing but her own. How
much better this serene if restricted joy than to
look across a normal street at " the people opposite,"
that always unsatisfactory variety of the human
species. The people opposite are capable of all—
they will set scarlet geraniums in array against yellow
calceolarias, and add pink penstemons and blue
lobelias to their " coloratura." They will hang
curtains which mimic the rosy fingers of Aurora at
windows which should be draped as with the snow-
white foam whence Aphrodite came.

From all such encounters and trials Sparrow-
crofters are protected. Could there be anything
more delightful than " a garden fornent the front
windows "? You leave the house, you cross the
thoroughfare, you enter your pleasance. There you
sit among your own flowers, seeing your own front
door, your own spotless, incomparable curtains.
All you see is yours. You agree with Berkeley that
" esse est percipi." What you do not see does not
exist for you. Rivalry is banished; complacency is
unchallenged; and Paradise is regained.

The Sparrowcroft gardens are small, about the
size of a quilt for the great Bed of Ware—and they
have almost every form of which a plane figure is
capable. Mrs Somerville would have delighted in
one which is an equilateral triangle, with its base

to the causeway and a red, red rose at its apex.
Another is rhomboidal and encloses a box-edged
circle of snapdragons, while a third relieves its
rectangular rigidity by topiarian effects in yew.
Only one of the gardens has clothes-poles, but there
seems a communal censorship which controls the
pendent results of the laundry.   Nausicaa herself
would have approved their purity, and no gar-
ment suggests such intimacy as would summon the
oriflamme to the cheek of any maiden.   The
delphiniums in the next garden seem to realize
that their azure spires gain brightness against the
fluttering whiteness, and they sway merrily in the
breeze which tosses them both.

Ornithologists tell me that sparrows are com-
bative and salacious, the very Don Juans and
Bobadils of the feathered world. But I cannot think
that Sparrowcroft harbours envies, quarrels, and
any inordinate motions and affections.   Minds
innocent and quiet take it for a hermitage.

Claverhouse ✑ ✑ ✑ ✑

WORDS in isolation are ambiguous. Teachers forget this when they ask their pupils' for " meanings " without giving a context. How different is the meaning of " interest " to a banker and to a librarian! How contrasting is the reaction of the word " overture " on a minister and on a musician! Who can declare the significance of " lawn " *per se*? Yet there is no uncertainty regarding Milton's

> *The shepherds on the lawn*
> *Or ere the point of dawn,*

or Shakespeare's

> *Lawn as white as driven snow.*

Shelley spoke a true word when he sang,

> *Nothing in this world is single.*

Ambiguity may dog denotation as well as connotation when a name is set in single unblessedness. The name " Paris " has a different reference for a student of the *Iliad* and for a modiste. " Dover " means to most of us the Kentish seaport, but it means to a nurse a sudorific powder.

All which is " prolegomena " to the statement that the title of this article does not refer to " the bloody Clavers," but to the barony in Angus where John Graham was born.

The lairdship of Claverhouse lies in Strathmartine on the left bank of the little River Dichty, a Sabbath day's journey from Dundee. Its seventeenth-century house has disappeared, but a later owner of the

112

estate built a sham ruin of castellated style, which credulous folk accept as the birthplace of the persecutor whose name has become " an astonishment and a hissing and a curse."

The Grahams may claim to equal the Campbells in their ability to " birze yont." Their cradle was in the Lennox by Fintry and Dundaff, and in Kincardine under the Ochils in ancient Fortrenn. They came into Angus when Robert the Bruce gave to a Graham the land of Auld Montrose in exchange for Cardross, on the Clyde, where the hero-king died. The Angus Grahams proliferated; I believe that is the proper biological term. There were Grahams of Morphie, Grahams of Duntrune, the last of whom was Miss Stirling Graham, of the *Mystifications*; Grahams of Fintry—a territorial designation transferred from Strathendrick to Strathdichty—one of whom made Burns a gauger, and Grahams of Claverhouse.

To-day Claverhouse means to the indwellers of Strathmartine one of the several bleach-fields on the Dichty. Those who see allegory where others see only accidentals may find it fitting that Claverhouse should be the scene of purifications. Mark Napier might agree, remembering his efforts to remove the spots of the leopard. Modern historians favour bleaching powders, but not all their chlorides have blanched the repute of the persecutor whom Habakkuk Mucklewrath summoned " to appear before the tribunal of God."

The Dichty is an alluring stream, such as Burns had in mind when he wrote,

> Now ower a linn the burnie plays. . . .
> Now cookit underneath the braes
> Below the spreadin' hazel.

That good Scots word " cookit," meaning " appeared and disappeared," is lost to the Scots vocabulary of to-day. The speech of modern Scottish

H

boys is bilingual, "A curn o' laddies," as they say in Angus, were on their way homeward from school, and were watching for trout in the Dichty. "See there's a big ane, aside the muckle stane," said one. English "big" and Scots "muckle," identical in meaning, were used in the same sentence.

The banks of the Dichty near Claverhouse are so thickly wooded that approach for angling or guddling is not easy. The river flows for a time under a long-drawn vault of verdure, which suggests how

> Alph, the sacred river, ran
> Through caverns measureless to man.

Trees are rare, however, on the braes that rise from the river towards the not distant Sidlaws. An occasional ash may be seen in a hedgerow or by a cotter's dwelling. Even on the last day of May the Claverhouse ash-trees were distrustful of snell winds and haar. They showed scarcely a leaf, meriting the reproof which Tennyson gave to their English sister,

> delaying, as the lingering ash delays,
> To clothe herself when all the woods are green.

The fields on the braes showed good red land, to the ploughing of which there had gone little whistling and much evident toil. The southern exposure set the soil free from the charge which Miss Stirling Graham brought against one of her farms that "it greets a' winter and girns a' simmer." One could not wish to see a better-wrought farm or a more bien steading than Barns of Claverhouse.

Will some psychologist tell me what variation of psychosis is indicated by the fact that Angus says Barns of Claverhouse and Barns of Wedderburn, which "marches" with it, while Lothian says Fenton Barns, Westbarns? In similar diversity the Highlands say Bridge of Allan, Bridge of Balgie,

Bridge of Tilt; while the Lowlands say Gorebridge, Coatbridge, Carronbridge. Like Rosa Dartle, I only ask for information.

The upper lands of Claverhouse afford a wide view to the southward. The conical hill, which an old ballad names, " The Law abune Dundee," but which is now within the city, gives a definite centre to the landscape as if it had been " composed " by Claude Lorraine. The Firth of Tay glitters behind it, and the hills of Fife, rising in the west to the Lomonds and the Ochils, form the back-cloth of the scene. Eastward the North Sea meets the horizon, and the mind's eye may traverse it with Sir Patrick Spens " to Norroway owre the faem."

Those upper acres of Claverhouse were in the seventeenth century broomy knowes and rough hill-pasture, and the laird of Claverhouse was a dealer in hides. The persecutor's grandfather, Sir William Graham of Claverhouse, agreed in 1602 with the magistrates of Dundee that he would test all hides, " baith rough and barkit," brought into the burgh, and would fix the prices to be charged for boots and shoes by the " cordiners." He was asked also to ordain penalties on " quha sall contravene and heicht the said prices." The relations of his grandson with the magistrates, after he obtained the constableship of Dundee, were not so friendly.

It is worth while noting for how brief a time John Graham held the title Viscount Dundee. He was raised to the peerage in November 1688, and died at Killiecrankie in July 1689. He may be said, however, to have had the best of it in his quarrel with the town, as he has filched from it the appellation, " Bonnie Dundee." The phrase was never applied to Graham of Claverhouse until Sir Walter Scott wrote his spirited verses describing Viscount Dundee's withdrawal from the Convention of Estates. It is used in several ballads about the

candle illumined all chemistry for Faraday's students; the earthworms led Darwin to the miracle of the earth's rejuvenescence and the unfailing resurgence of its harvests. Teachers may travel from any moment or scene of the usual day farther than Phæthon drove, and with better fortune. Only they must be convinced of the highway wisdom of Stevenson that to travel is better than to arrive, and the teacher who sets out to plough with the heifer of Jacotot must be, as Compayré warned, " très-instruit et très-experimenté."

Such thoughts jostled each other in my mind as I passed along a street which seemed to " feature " only the surface interests of a fleeting time. Cinemas, confectioners', drapers' garish windows, the occluded lights of billiard saloons, the tyrannical odours of fish resisting their submergence in torrid and partly clarified fat—from which of these may the spirit leap to comprehension of the intensity and the range of man? Here surely the wheels of the Jacotot-chariot drive heavily, and no star glimmers whereunto one may hitch a wagon. But the dullest street has its sudden turnings, and a corner may reveal a vista as full of promise as that from Pisgah. So it is here, for the next corner discloses a church-yard gateway, and occasion to try our Jacotot-wings. Surely that portal was reared by Adam, not him of Eden but him of the Adelphi. Only our Scots Palladio, or at least some Adamite pupil, could have devised those pillars. They are no mere superincumbent loads, but rise from the earth and bear equally their crowning vases, on which the ornament is adequate yet of that restraint of which Adam, of the Adelphi, had the secret and of which Adam, of Paradise, made no trial, to our woe and loss of Eden. What influences from the sands below Ravensheuch and the cliffs where " Alisaundre our King was deid " moulded the soul of Robert Adam to a skill in monumental mass unequalled since Wren, and to an aptitude of decorative grace as if he had lingered in the studio of Watteau or had seen the clay take life under the fingers of Jean Goujon? London is being rebuilt to-day in the Adam tradition, but what Kirkcaldy schoolboy knows the works and days of the greatest Scots artist in form? What citizen of the Lang Toon ever goes "anes errand" to gaze on Adam's *chefs-d'œuvres*, the Register House and Charlotte Square. The old Adam is too strong: Adam Smith, architect of economics, is more honoured than Robert Adam, architect of edifices. Yet the system to which the economist furnished a logic is tottering around us to-day while the buildings for which the artist drew the plans stand fast yet as Craigellachie, except in Glasgow.

But let us enter the churchyard, not to wag a moralizing lip among its neglected tombs nor to survey the church which the Nine Trades reared and girt about with lairs, since it is becoming well together such as brethren are in unity to dwell when hearing sermons, or when Death, the final Deacon of all crafts, bids all tools yield to a pickaxe and a spade.

Our objective is that hexagonal building beyond the churchyard wall with the moulded rybats on its Romanesque windows. It is now a timber store; the sexton will tell you it was "the kail kirk," and in it are entombed the hopes of John Glas who, early in the eighteenth century, had faith that what Paul had planted and Apollos watered had need of his pruning to secure its increase. An origin from Auchtermuchty and Galloway, a boyhood in Kinclaven Manse, a lear-time in St Johnston and St Andrews, brought him in 1719 as minister to the Angus parish of Tealing. He that will to Tealing goes to Tealing, for it leads nowhither. He that dwells in Tealing may from its seclusion lift up his eyes unto the hills and may trace on the eastern horizon where great sea-billows are. But unless he is very dull or very " hard ca'ed," he will find great zones of leisure engirdling his days as navigators by the Galapagos find belts of calms. John Glas had wide periods of vacuity, and golf was as yet a maritime triviality for the senescent, so he set himself, as if his birth had been at Berea rather than at the back of the Lomonds, to search the Scriptures from the rising of the sun over Murroes to its going down behind Craigowl. So, to their honour be it said, did most of his fellow-presbyters throughout Scotland, but with a difference. They read their Bibles to find support for the beliefs they already held. The eident and evangelical Boston of Ettrick, and his opponents in the Marrow Controversy, draw the weapons they use against each other from the same armoury. John Glas pored over the sacred page to discover *its* views. He was, of course, as a mariner before the compass was known or a star-gazer before Copernicus came. Richard Simon had made in France a beginning of Biblical criticism, but Bossuet, the Eagle of Meaux, had used his talons against the critic and in the realm of apologetics and history could spread his broad wings un-challenged and supreme. John Glas's patient study, in its narrow literalness, the same mental habitude in which he had studied his *Corderius*, brought him at last to question if the Church of Scotland were identical, in rites and rule, in doctrine and discipline, with the Church of the New Testament. As a true-blue Scot he had been convinced from his youth up that the Church of Rome was established on the sands and that the Church of England had no sure foundation on its shifting shingle. But could it be that the Church of Scotland, the purest kirk in Christendom, as King James had called it, as firm on the rock as Alclyd, Snowdoun and Dunedin on

their crags, could she too have varied from her
primal original? That was a tense hour in the
manse study at Tealing, and I think I see John Glas
rise from his chair, pace the narrow room, and look
from the window upon the quiet glebe and sleeping
kirkton to still his beating mind.

Differences and variations have no terrors for us
to-day. We armour ourselves with theories, or at
least phrases, of evolution, of necessary mutations,
of morphological variation, as proof of an unvarying
"élan vital," of being as assured only by its
relativity in becoming, and of a time-conditioned
sequence of institutional phases of the eternal flux.
M. de Loisy and Dean Inge knew that " they didn't
know everything down in Judee," and would have
smiled at John Glas's perturbations. But John Glas
was a simple man, unable to make the worse appear
the better reason, and he spoke out his uncertainties
to his parishioners, his presbytery, and in prolix
pamphlets which the chapmen sold from the bundles
in which they were tied up along with *Lothian Tam*,
Blind Harry, and *Eppie of Buckhaven*. Peasant life
was arduous in Angus; the cold soil greets a' winter
and girns a' simmer; men needed some relief from
the toils of runrig, and they took their pleasures
ardently in theological debate. The Shirramuir
was nearly forgotten, and Angus has always dearly
loved boldness and a scandal. It was little wonder,
therefore, that the heretical minister of Tealing was
talked of in Dundee when market-days were wearin'
late, and bargaining was over. Yet, after all, Glas's
variations were very slight. He denied the perpetual
obligation of covenant-making, to the horror of the
MacMillanites and his Galloway kin; he questioned
the power of the civil magistrate in religious affairs;
he urged the restoration of the kiss of peace with
which the apostle bade Christians salute each
other; he maintained the duty of the weekly

" agape " or love-feast, which prevailed in the early
Church. He did not accept the Eucharist as its
substitute, least of all in the Scots practice of a
half-yearly Sacrament, or a yearly Holy Fair.
To-day, he would probably have been of those who
accept the teaching of M. Bossuet in *Kurios Christos*,
or of M. Guignebert, and the school which traces
Christian ritual to the mystery-religion of the East
more than to apostolic sanction. His presbytery
suspended him; the Synod of Angus and Mearns
confirmed the judgment, and the General Assembly
deposed him in 1729. The Church of Scotland
at that time was in full accord with the spirit of
Talleyrand's dictum of later days, " Surtout, pas de
zèle ! " And the General Assembly had its hand in
at deposing ministers, as the Relief and the Secession
learned. Glas removed to Dundee, a city ever
receptive of schisms and enamoured of frankness,
and gathered a congregation which practised the
" agape," meeting for a common meal every
Sabbath. From this usage the dwellers in the
Bucklemaker Wynd and others called the new
" ecclesia " the kail kirk. What power, and often
what unfairness, lies in an epithet. Even in *The
Dictionary of National Biography* you will find " John
Glas, a Scottish Sectary," as if he had been a mere
troubler of Israel. Glas gained many followers, and
Duncan Forbes of Culloden eloquently urged the
General Assembly not to proceed to extremities
against a devout and zealous minister because of
" speculative tendencies." Forbes was one of those
who suggest Chaucer's line, " Pity runneth soon in
gentle heart." Butcher Cumberland called him
" that old woman who spoke to me of humanity."
One of the reasons why some of us would like to
believe with Dante and Milton in Inferno, and its
adamantine chains and penal fire, is that otherwise
Cumberland and his like will never meet their

deserts. It is the more to Culloden's credit that he pleaded for Glas, as his own theological leanings lay in other directions from Glas's hard literalness of Biblical interpretation. As one looks in Parliament House on the fine statue of Culloden by Roubilliac, it is not easy to understand his inclination to what was known as Hutchinsonianism, which declared the Bible to be inerrant, but explained all troublesome passages as allegory and symbol. Hutchinson had gained notoriety and a government sinecure, when Newton issued his *Principia*, by publishing *Moses' Principia*, a defence of the Mosaic cosmogony, and an attack on the theory of gravitation. Glas had more scholarship than Hutchinson, but less volubility and good fortune. The brightest gleam came when his daughter, after his removal to Perth, married Robert Sandeman, who wedded with equal eagerness the Glassite doctrines. Sandeman bore them to Edinburgh, and then, like bonny Leslie, ga'ed across the Border to spread their conquest further. The new sect, known more often as Sandemanians, prospered in London. Sandeman himself had the gangin' foot, and went to America, where several congregations were established. In the turmoils before the Declaration of American Independence Sandeman was a strong opponent of the Colonials, and was embroiled in many troubles. So rarely do those who have achieved freedom for themselves show eagerness to permit liberty to others. It is a far cry from Dundee to Philadelphia, but thus far may a little candle throw its beams, and thus closely may Tealing be linked with Ticonderoga.

The romance of John Glas's life lies in his mental adventures, his intellectual explorations, the outfaring of his soul in search of truth. George Glas, his son, a native of Dundee, knew in his different life the more accepted yet not more wondrous romance of external vicissitudes, the traversing of remote lands, and the fellowship of mysterious races. Trained as a surgeon, he made several voyages to the West Indies, and might have vied with Smollett in depicting the ugliness and the discomforts of the Esculapian life on the ocean wave. He explored the African coast between Capes Bojador and Blanco and sought to claim the hinterland for Britain. The Spaniards imprisoned him at Tenerife, but the British Government, from whom he had strong though unavowed support, secured his release. Accompanied by his wife and daughter Glas set sail for England in a ship whose crew included many Spaniards and Portuguese. A wild tale that the ship was bearing vast treasure to England excited the cupidity of the credulous dagoes, and, off the coast of Ireland, they mutinied. Glas was stabbed, his wife and daughter were thrown overboard, and the mutineers, scuttling the ship, took to the boats with their scanty plunder and a specious tale of the hazards of the sea. But best-laid schemes gang agley, especially in Ireland. The ship drifted ashore, and its decks, red with carnage, revealed the truth. The mutineers were captured roystering in a roadside tavern and were hanged in Dublin. George Glas was a scholar in the speech of Castile and Lusitania; he translated *The History of the Canary Islands*, and on his last voyage was busy writing an account of N.W. Africa. Full fathoms five under the waves of Elreann lies the son of the Kail Kirk who had paidled in the Tod's Burn and pu'd the gowans by the Chapelshade Braes. His father was laid under good Scots clods in Perth. Whose lot, in life, in death, would you choose? Which world, that of thought or that of action, offers the stranger hazards or the further faring from the ways of youth? " Tout est dans tout," and the evening brings all home.

Saint Cuthbert's Town ᕽ   ᕽ

AYTOUN in one of his "Blackwood" tales tells of an Englishman who would not believe that there was a town with such a name as Clackmannan. I am sure there are Englishmen and others who have refrained from visiting Kirkcudbright because they did not know how to say its name. There is more in a name than Juliet guessed, and St Cuthbert's would have started another spirit than Kirkcudbright, which is but a false archaism. The Lammermuir laddie who became the great saint who sleeps at Durham was Cudbeorht or Cuthbeorht. "Beorht" is Old English for bright, and someone with this dangerous little learning is responsible for the present spelling of the name of the pleasant town by the southern Dee. The south country prefers the Kirk-form in its place names. It has Kirkoswald, Kirkbride, Kirkpatrick, Kirkmaiden, Stephenkirk (Steenykirk), which ignorance has spoiled to Stoneykirk, while the north of Forth prefers St Andrews, St Fillans, St Cyrus.

By whatever name Kirkcudbright was called, and however oddly its name was spelled, it is one of the most delightful places in Scotland. Hills, river, woods, and sea combine to give it an aspect and environment of ceaseless charm. Nor is the town unworthy of its situation. There are wide airy streets, frequent aspiring towers, quaint pends, the dignified lodgings of Galloway lairds who passed their winters there, an ancient castle, and a Tolbooth which lifts a pleasing tower to the Galloway sky. Would that those who built the new Academy had looked longer at the Tolbooth and had managed to give the school some of the individuality and vigour of the ancient building! And why, since Kirkcudbright has keepit a schule since the twelfth century, does she ca' it an Academy?

Something of the air of a cathedral city, something of an academic aspect, marks Kirkcudbright. In St Mary's Garden or under the pends the flash of a scarlet gown, as at St Andrews, would be in harmony. And one listens for the drowsy booming of a minster clock as one saunters under the overarching trees that lead towards Dundrennan. Kirkcudbright is a dignified town, and I am puzzled why Burns, who personified Lochmaben so nobly as "Marjorie o' the Mony Lochs," should have given to Kirkcudbright the uncouth prosopopœia of

> *Brandy Jean that took her gill*
> *In Galloway sae wide.*

The exciseman spoke there, not the poet.

To natural beauty and grace of aspect, Kirkcudbright adds the potent appeal of historical associations, numerous, varied and alluring. The Toom Tabard, the Red Comyn, and the Hammer of the Scots have harboured in its castle. Claverhouse and his dragoons have raced through its Meikle Yett under the spiked heads of the martyrs of the Covenant. You may pass up to Tongland and, if you can avert your eyes from the beauty of the wooded gorge of the Dee, you may recall the "Fenzeit Friar of Tongland," whom Dunbar pilloried, the first attempter of aviation in Scotland. Or you may pass down to St Mary's Isle, once "Prioratus Sanctæ Mariæ de Trayl," and recall its former prior, David Paniter, of whom Knox says: "Eating and drinking was all his pastyme." His Latin letters to foreign potentates while he was secretary to three successive Scots monarchs were published and praised by Ruddiman. So Paniter must have laboured as well as had pastime.

Or you may prefer to recall rather the gardener's son of Arbigland, John Paul, the co-worker with Washington and Hamilton and Lafayette in the freeing of the United States. As Paul Jones, he laughed at Britannia's claim to rule the waves, affrighted the coasts of England and Scotland, and carried off the Earl of Selkirk's silver plate from St Mary's Isle. Eager that the new republic should not imitate the monarchic practice of loot, Benjamin Franklin secured its restoration to that branch of the Douglases. When one remembers how Paul Jones taught America the importance of sea-power and that an Earl of Selkirk from St Mary's Isle founded Manitoba, one is surprised that Americans have not added Kirkcudbright to the Trossachs and Edinburgh and Melrose Abbey as a place of pilgrimage.

Most visitors are contented to see in MacLellan's Castle the chief historic interest in Kirkcudbright. I wish the MacLellans would decide what is the proper form of their name—MacLellan, MacClellan, or MacClelland. I wish no one would confuse them with Highland MacLennans. The MacLellans were of Bombie, five miles away, but built their fine fortress-house in Kirkcudbright in 1582. They had warred with and for the Douglases, and, if legend speak truth, against that subtler foe, the Galloway gipsies, but they were seldom prosperous. They always chose the wrong moment for changing sides, becoming King's men when the blue banner of the Covenant was victorious everywhere, and turning to the Covenant just before the King came to his own again. One was made Lord Kirkcudbright in 1633 by Charles I., but Charles II. stripped his grandson of his estates, and the family sank into poverty. Oliver Goldsmith, when he was a student of medicine at Edinburgh, saw a Lord Kirkcudbright who kept a glove-shop. Goldsmith jeered at the pride and poverty of the Scottish nobles. Kirk-cudbright's ancestors had been more familiar no doubt with gloves of steel. I suspect in Goldsmith's reference, however, the rancour of one who had been refused gloves unless he paid for them, a condition of possession which Goldsmith was rarely willing to fulfil.

Artists resort in coveys to Kirkcudbright, and you will hear in its inns much talk of Cézanne and Van Gogh and of the errors of representationism. It may be a fanciful thought, but the atmosphere of Galloway and the Solway shore seems to me to have more of that pearly radiance of the French landscape than other regions of Scotland. There the enthusiast of pleinairism and post-impressionism will find scope for their efforts and incitement to their theories. There the eye is enchanted by the sweet freshness of the morning on river and meadow, by glade and glen. There the eye falls at evening on silver mists and tenuous shadows such as only Corot's brush could limn with their own delicacy. Nowhere will the artist find more alluring subjects, nowhere will they evade his skill more tantalizingly, than in St Cuthbert's Town.

Kilmany ⌒ ⌒ ⌒ ⌒

THE kingdom by the sea which men call Fife is not less notable for its diversity than for its record and its sons. Gaul, that was divided into but three parts, was a homogeneous monotony compared with the kaleidoscopic land that lies below the Lomonds and ripples between Forth and Tay. Consider but what differences of aspect, of history, and of life's trend are suggested by St Andrews and Lumphinnans, by Kilconquhar and Halbeath, by Falkland, Saline, Pickletillem, Lathones and Cardenden. Little wonder the Fifer is shrewd, familiar from his youth with *tot discrimina rerum*, the affairs of Balmerino and Moss Morran, Crail, Ceres and Dunfermline, Kirkcaldy and Carnbee.

The Kingdom is rather weak in regional naming, although the East Neuk and the Howe of Fife have a definite range. I know no name for the section which margins Tay from ancient Abernethy and Macduff's Cross to where St Francis would have been happy among the birds on Tents Muir.

The surface of this latter region is like a basket of eggs. Hog-backed, green hills of moderate height huddle together, like cows in a loan at gloaming, and in their valleys one strays to devious courses, constrained by the variant slopes, and conscious of a restricted sky. Who keeps on the ridges has his eye led eastward to the ocean, or north and westward to the giant bens. Who keeps to the valleys is teased by solicitations to a' the airts. With whom does wisdom dwell, with him, the man of one idea, one interest, one gift, who makes his life tread a

clear highway to achievement or success? Or with
him, whom men call mutable, for whom Bypath
Meadow is ever alluring, and *quicquid homines agunt*
draws diversely the gaze and energy of his mind?
Such thoughts, as prevaricating as the response of
an ancient oracle, beset my mind as I made my
way from The Gauldry to see the kirk at Kilmany,
from which Dr Chalmers fulmined over Scotland
more than a century ago. As I set out, I had been
pondering why map-makers with evil unanimity
denude place-names of the article when they have
a right to that distinction. Everyone in Fife says
The Gauldry, The Elie, The Star, as everyone in
Lothian says The Stow, and everyone in Cunningham, The Largs. Yet cartographers commit their
vile aphæresis unchecked and unabashed. What
Frenchman would endure to see Le Havre, Le Mans,
La Rochelle, thus cropped? I would imprison such
amputators on The Bass or The May until they had
purged their offence against the articles, and I would
make The Chisholm their judge and compurgator.

Kilmany is the Church of Monan, the companion
of St Odhran in preaching the Gospel to Fife. His
relics, borne to the Church of Abercrombie, that
cliff-built rugged fane over which the spindrift flies,
drew such devotion that the name of the parish is
gone, and church and village are St Monans unto
this day. Those who sought their harvest on the
wild waves, and those who filled their girnels from
the quiet fields beneath Murdochcairnie, alike
reverenced the good Monan, who told them of Him
who chose fishermen as His disciples, and seed-time
and harvest as parables for His teaching. Perhaps
even St Monan, and certainly Dr Chalmers, would
yet recognize Kilmany. The highway and the rail-
road rush past it, but the clachan of red-tiled
cottages heeds neither. It spreads its aippleringie
and golden-rod, its profuse and evanescent white

roses on the little hillock crowned by the kirk as in the days when Dr Chalmers rode down the slope, with a tumble at every mile, to lecture on mathematics or chemistry at St Andrews, and defy the moderator of his presbytery when the fathers and brethren suggested restriction of his energies to religion and his cure.

There is no poem by a Scottish poet at all comparable, at least in subject, to Gray's *Elegy*, although Blair in *The Grave* has parallel passages to the English poet's moralizing on " the inevitable hour." Burns avoids the kirkyaird except as a background, and Stevenson but makes it a foil to the service and the congregation in *The Lowden Sabbath Morn*. Is this avoidance due to its being as difficult usually to get into a Scots kirk on a weekday as for a rich man to enter the kingdom of heaven? I was more fortunate, for Kilmany kirk was " takin' in coals," and all access was as open as if *St George's, Edinburgh*, had been sung. The church is a plain parallelogram with a bell-cote, owing any grace it has to its lichened age. It is long and narrow, with the pulpit on the long south wall, and east and west lafts. Most of the congregation therefore must see the minister mainly in profile, an aspect not the most favouring to an average Scots face. The minister must, if he wishes to hold his hearers with a glittering eye, keep his head pivoting around a semicircle. I suggested that inconvenience to the beadle, who replied, " This yin jist looks straucht forrit."

The only relic associated with Dr Chalmers is the sand-glass, which was formerly on the pulpit, and measured to the sermon-lovers the brevity of their joy and to the heedless the approach of their release.

The fame of the orator is the most immediate yet the most insubstantial variety of renown. Later ages cannot confute it, though they may marvel at the dreary ashes which represent what record declares to have been jets of blazing lava. Scotland is pre-eminently the land of sermons, yet if we except the archaic quaintnesses of Robert Bruce and Thomas Boston, what remains to interest a student from all the pulpit eloquence that has been displayed in print? One may yet be stirred on reading the sermons of Bossuet and Massillon as their first auditors at Versailles were stirred. One may read with profit and pleasure the sermons of Robertson of Brighton, and with a differing, yet satisfying, appreciation the sermons of Canon Liddon. But not even a moderator marooned through a wet week in August in a manse on Mingulay but would yawn and be aweary, weary, if he had set out to read through Blair's *Sermons*, Logan's *Sermons*, Chalmers' *Sermons*. When I turn over the pages of Dr Chalmers' *Sermons*, or read the extracts in that dull book, *Memoirs of Dr Chalmers*, which is mere mummied remains, with no vital presentation of the man—in brief, a life written by a son-in-law —I am inclined to wonder if the Chalmers' legend has any other basis than verbosity and vehemence, and if the rustic whose comment was, " The fro' was fleein' frae his mooth like sixpences," had not explained its origin. But J. G. Lockhart was not to be overwhelmed by mere noise, and the tribute to Dr Chalmers in the third volume of *Peter's Letters to his Kinsfolk* is of such a character that one is forced to acknowledge the greatness of the personality which could make so impressive the sermons which are so empty to read. It were perhaps to inquire too curiously to ask if eloquence which diverts the mind mainly to admiration of the orator is in its fit place in the pulpit. Cowper had no doubt on the matter when he wrote:

> *Or will he seek to dazzle me with tropes,*
> *And play his brilliant parts before my eyes,*
> *When I am hungry for the bread of life?*

Lockhart, himself a minister's son, and familiar with all the difficulties of a preacher's task, as *Adam Blair* shows, finds in Chalmers no such *hybris*, and rejoices in the evidence of a true pastoral relation to the congregation of St John's Church, Glasgow. In his study of Henry Cockburn as an advocate Lockhart has a fine phrase which would meet Cowper's plaint, and may be commended to all probationers and selection committees in vacant charges: " It is not his ambition to be admired: he wishes only to be trusted." There is no doubt, however, that the influence of Chalmers turned Scottish preaching towards rhetoric and sesquipedalian verbiage. Stevenson had heard much of such echoing rotundity. He was of the Auld Kirk, which was faithful to the Chalmers' tradition when the Free Kirk showed rather the intoned fervour and anacoloutha which were its tribute to MacCheyne, and from his memories he made his line of fit description:

> *The braw words rummle ower the heid,*
> *Nor steer the sleeper.*

Most of us reveal ourselves in our *obiter dicta*. Dr Chalmers was in Edinburgh at the visit of George IV., and was displeased at the tepidity of the welcome given to that disreputable Guelph. It may be doubted if Edinburgh would have applauded more resonantly even Aristides. " Why are you not more vociferous? " he said to one who stood by him in the crowd. " Vociferous " is the word which describes himself and his style. He writes to his father in rolling periods appropriate to a public meeting. In a letter to a sister, one compound sentence, occupying sixteen lines of print, contains three principal clauses, each with a train of subordinate clauses, the second having six such, with subordinate or parenthetical clauses interspersed.

We of to-day are asthmatical and short-winded in utterance compared with the breathers of such stentorian longinquity. The letter was written just after his marriage, and the bridegroom tells his sister, " I meet with nothing but the most cheerful and delightful concurrence." Why should such a sentence raise a smile, while we are moved only to admiration by the poet's expression of the same thought: " Two minds with but a single thought, two hearts that beat as one "? To understand that would be to solve the problem of style. One wants to say to those who use such words as " concurrence " and " homologate " Caliban's curse — " The red plague rid you for learning me your language ! " But Kilmany, bonnie Kilmany, with its peaceful churchyard, should not be made an Ebal, least of all on this peaceful evening at the hint o' hairst. So I shall only smile at the oddity of some good men, and the flaws of style in the great and good Dr Chalmers, as I retrace my steps by The Gauldry, and see the sunset over Dunsinane burnish the waters of the Tay.

Accidentals ∽ ∽ ∽ ∽

THE chief interest of a book should lie in its contents. Apples are the main justification of the apple-tree. Yet one may find allurement in the study of its parasitic mistletoe in biology and in myth, and the legend of Eve's bite may be refreshing as any munching of the fruit. A concern with the accidentals of books needs no apology unless it displaces the study of them. Youth seldom cares for such things. Its lust for reading rages; its thirst for experience, even if it be only imaginative experience, is unslaked. Youth is naturally scornful of those, collectors rather than readers, who value books for their rarity, their misprints, their origin from Plantin types or the Doves Press or " Glasguae; in academicis ædibus excudebant Robertus et Andreas Foulis," their Grolier binding, their publication " apud Danielem Elzevirium " or by Pickering, and all the other whims and obsessions of the bibliomaniac. The dream and the business of youth is to collect vibrations; the middle years, which are rather weary of emotions, and even of thought, begin to find a charm in externalities and slacken, it may be, in their reading, to gossip about the parasitic interests of a library. Only the wealthy can be collectors nowadays, but all who gather books may have volumes with interesting " accidentals."

Here is Calderwood's *History of the Church of Scotland*, neighbouring on the shelf the same author's *Altare Damascenum*. I take the former down sometimes because it was printed before the Revolution at some secret press in Holland, and shows no place of imprint. Its fly-leaf bears the shield and autograph of the Earl of Orrery, son, I think, of the earl after whom the celestial mechanism was named, and great-grandson of the first earl, the brother of the proclaimer of Boyle's Law, and governor of resentful Scotland for Cromwell as well as writer of romances and comedies for the courtiers of Charles II. The book is thus to me, as it were, a ganglion at which intertwine associates of chemistry and the Covenant, playwrights and Puritans, the follies of man and his glory. The first Earl of Orrery, to our great loss, never wrote of his experiences in Scotland, but there must have been talk of them in the family, since the third generation took trouble to bind beautifully the bold and unlicensed volume of the champions of the Kirk and the blue banner.

On the shelf below is a slim book, *Notes on Modern Theories of Morals*. One of my own professors wrote it, but I no longer believe that introspection will reveal the origin of ethical values. Historical research has restricted the speculation in which moralists revelled. Yet I sometimes turn its pages, because the book belonged to Herbert Spencer and because I like to wonder what that philosopher said at certain stages of the argument. When the book became mine, the pages were uncut beyond about the middle. There is a tale of a French writer who read one of his works to a famous critic. In the course of the reading the critic fell asleep. The author protested "You promised me your opinion and you have fallen asleep." The critic's reply was "Sleep also is an opinion." The uncut pages seemed to me a dramatic and decisive opinion from Spencer.

Here is an edition of the poems of the Sempills of Beltrees. Has it any accidental of interest? It was published in Edinburgh at 87 Prince's Street in 1849. All the world writes Princes Street now, and most visitors regard the name as if it were *La Rue des Princes*. My book reminds me that it was *La Rue du Prince*. " Cette fameuse terrasse," as M. Paul Bourget called it, commemorates the worthless prince who was afterwards George IV., as George Street, which old-fashioned folk still call George's Street, commemorates his father, and Queen Street, whence Scottish churches and schools are ruled, commemorates his dull and rigid mother. These are the three Graces of the Edinburgh streets; Princes Street a heroine of romance, alluring and enchanted; George Street, a stately matron of opulent dignity; Queen Street, whom there are very few to praise as she deserves, a gracious silence like Virgilia, a kind of Sister Anne gazing wistfully to see if anyone is coming frae the north to fancy her, and yet with sudden thrills of heart as, like the Greeks of the *Anabasis*, she gains glimpses of " Thalassa ! Thalassa ! "

There may be something to be said for the music of *Rule, Britannia!* but little praise can be given to the windy words. I should be pleased enough if responsibility for them could be transferred from Thomson, the poet of *The Seasons*, to David Mallet. Mallet softened his name from Malloch when he went among the weak-throated English of the south. His clan should have punished him for his degeneracy, as Jael did Sisera, with a nail and a mallet. My copy of Mallet's poems has a facsimile of the receipt which he gave for his half-year's salary as janitor of the High School of Edinburgh. One used to think that the beadle of a church had to be a very good man, since the Psalm said, "Rather in the Lord's house will I keep a door than dwell in tents of sin." To keep a door in a school does not require one to be a good poet, but the salary was in the true poetic tradition "Ten pounds Scots money as a half years aliment due to me from

lambmas 1717 to Candlemas last by past 1718."
The receipt is given to the " thesaurer " of the city
of Edinburgh, a majestic word which we lost, as
Andrew Fairservice would have said, " through the
sorrowfu' Union."   When Mallet married an
English lady with ten thousand pounds, and hob-
nobbed with and was pensioned by Prince " Fred
who was alive and is dead," I wonder if he ever
thought of comparing the swift rush of his prosperity,
and the swelling praises the critics gave his verses,
to the Lammas Floods. I fear that after he drew up
with Englishers and success he forgot the Hieland
hills that were far awa' and the janitor's experiences
at *Schola Regia Edinburgensis*.

A Scot of the same century and similar momentary
renown was James Beattie, whom Johnson honoured
as a poet, and mole-eyed minds declared to have
" answered Hume " in philosophy. When I am
irritated by the formless, rhythmless, meaningless
collocations of words which often to-day are ac-
claimed as great Georgian poetry, I calm myself
by remembering that equally extravagant and less
baseless laudation was given to the over-regularized
conventional verbosity of Beattie and others in the
eighteenth century, and that it has all gone into
the wallet of oblivion. My copy of Beattie's *Minstrel*
has an accidental that is more poetical than any of
his lines. Its flyleaf bears the following inscription,
" Filiæ dilectæ, nec satis unquam diligendæ, Harriet
Turner, hocce libellum, D.D.   Dawson Turner,
grati animi testimonium, Virgilii Eneide intra
quindecim menses memoriæ mandata: Yarmutha
Kal. Dec. MDCCCXXI." I do not know whether
to admire more the memorizing powers of the
daughter or the exultant pride of the father or
the columnar arrangement of the inscription or the
underlying implication that there is a community
between Beattie and Virgil! David Copperfield

was travelling in Barkis's cart to Yarmouth when Harriet Turner was committing the *Æneid* to memory. So diverse are the lots of mortals. The proud father was evidently not very sure what was the Latin for Yarmouth. His word looks most like *Yarmutha*, but the last letter is blotted, a device by which boys in all generations have tried to veil their ignorance of a case ending in *a*. Mediæval monks no doubt wrote things like *Yarmutha*, but a lover of Virgil should rather have tried after something like *Ostium Garense*.

In the next book the accidental which catches my eye is the date. The book is bound in tree-calf with gilt tooling and is entitled *Le Nouvel Homme*. It was published " à Paris chez les Directeurs de l'Imprimerie du Cercle Social, L'An quatrième de la Liberté." It reminds me, therefore, that the French Revolutionists abolished the Christian era, as they transformed the calendar, and sought to make the world date its history from the year of the Revolution, "l'an de la Liberté." The piquant circumstance is that the book *Le Nouvel Homme* is a volume of pious exhortation and religious meditations in what one might fairly call the Jansenist tradition, of a fervour and intimacy of appeal such as suggests to a Scot the writings of Samuel Rutherford or Lady Culross or Robert Murray MacCheyne. Not all France was worshipping at the festival of reason when such a book was published freely. I will not say I have read the book through, but I look now and again at the final sentence, " Toutes les merveilles de la Jérusalem céleste peuvent se retrouver encore aujourd'hui dans le cœur du nouvel homme"; and sometimes I smile and sometimes I sigh.

When I take up the next book I turn to the end, for its last leaf bears the signature of Andrew Fletcher of Saltoun. That Scots patriot is little remembered, and his descendants cast his library to the bookstalls. A chance reader may recall his saying, variously expressed, that he cared not who made the laws of a nation if he might but make its ballads. All the philosophy of education is in that sentence, and it is significant that Fletcher owned the *De Disciplinis* of Ludovicus Vives, the Spanish humanist, who taught classics at Louvain and embodied much of the best thought of the Renaissance in this book. Below Fletcher's autograph an earlier owner of the book, for the script is of an earlier style, has written Ludovicus twice, misspelling it Lodovicus, and underneath " Lord have mercy." There is wide scope for the fancy to surmise to what the prayer refers.

When I turned up a *Dictionary of Eminent Scotsmen*, the only Fraser noted was Simon Fraser, the notorious Lord Lovat, who has attracted so many historians and novelists, though none has been able to make his strange story credible to our understanding. The Dictionary was unfair to a noble clan, and might at least have included the Reverend James Fraser of Brea, laird and minister, Covenanting prisoner on The Bass and writer of what the highflyers of the eighteenth century called marrowy spiritual memoirs. Here they are in the Gaelic, which was his mother-speech, with himself disguised to the Lowlander as Urr. Seumas Frisael, Braighe. I am accustomed to write down together the Lowland Brea and the Gaelic Braighe when I want to call the attention of a teacher to the consonants of a vanished utterance which abound in Gaelic words and, more often, when I am fretted by hearing children who are studying the magic straits by the shores of Skye speaking of the Sound of Sleat, as if its name rhymed with treat. It rhymes with gate, as Brea rhymes with gay, which the reverend James seldom was, and not with flee, which as a Fraser he would not do.

All these accidentals are adventitious interests which the books have added to themselves in the hazard of their continuance and the mutations of their ownership. They have little relation to the contents, and deal with things of the past. Only last week, however, a modern book added an accidental to itself. It is a volume of the poetry of Mr W. B. Yeats, with a beautiful Celtic design on the binding, tooled lavishly with gold. I spoke of it to Mr Yeats, who replied, " Let me tell you the story of the designer of the binding." She was a daughter of a West of Ireland great family who quarrelled with her people and betook herself in revolt to Dublin to study art. She had jewels which she pawned, for she was thus far modern. These gave her an income of about five shillings a week, on which it was possible to exist in Dublin twenty-five years ago. But she was also so *de l'ancien régime* that no woman of her family had ever gone unattended on the streets of a town. Though she could quarrel with her relatives, she could not break with the convention, or rather with the malaise which breach of the tradition meant to her mind. So half of the weekly five shillings was spent on hiring an old woman to walk beside her on the streets of Dublin, as had been the usage of the Joyces of Joycetown—that was not her name— since the time of the Wild Geese or the days of the Five Masters. She made progress in her art, and her design for Mr Yeats's book was accepted by the London publisher. Friends secured her a commission to make some drawings for an architect. She brought them to Mr Yeats and said she felt they were inartistic. The architect was pleased, however, and paid her for the drawings, but asked her to make some slight modifications. She spent all the money, and came to Mr Yeats to tell him some days after that she had burned the drawings.

" They were not yours after you had been paid for them," said the poet, " I call that theft." " So do I," replied the artist, " and all night long I have lain awake pondering which is the greater crime, the crime against Art to allow these drawings to continue, or the crime against Society in my spending money for which I can give nothing. I have decided that a crime against Art is the unpardonable sin, compared with which a crime against Society is but venial." Such a story reveals the greatness and the strangeness of the Irish mind, its marvellous acuteness and its power of overwhelming in some sudden surge of idealism the motives which more prudent individuals and a duller race regard as the firm poles of action. I shall never again look at that volume without remembering the story of that Irish girl artist. And for all the charms of Innisfree, and the ardours of Grania with the burning hair, I thought as I listened to Mr Yeats how strange it was that poets should deem the romance of phantoms by the cromlech and apparitions in the glen more wonderful than the romance of character and temperament in the real men and women whom their own eyes behold.

Scotticisms ∽ ∽ ∽ ∽

Traps for the Scot Abroad

MRS PRINGLE in *The Ayrshire Legatees* laments, " This great London is but a bare place efter a': there's no a jigot o' mutton to be got in the hale toon." She might have added, " nor an ashet on which to serve it." The Scot who " hauds sooth " nowadays is not likely to expect his vernacular to be understood on the banks of Thames. Though he choose his words as delicately as Agag came, he is likely enough to use Scotticisms at which the Southron will titter. He will probably write home to Kennaquhair, " I knew I was in England whenever I came to Carlisle," or " I had a pleasant companion the length of York." A Scot who had " come back " gave to a forth-faring Scot two rules, " Never say to a Londoner, ' Will I open the window? ' for he'll laugh at you; and never say, ' I don't mind what you said,' for he'll be angry with you." For " mind," which means " remember " in Scots, means " heed " in English.

The real difficulty of the exile is his discovery that even the good English of Scotland is not *English* English. If he speak of the " forenoon" he will be met with a stare of astonishment, and perhaps by a challenge. It will avail not to cite Shakespeare as his exemplar. The morning and the evening are the day in London, as in Genesis, and the morning has annexed all the A.M. territory, though Scotland yet recognizes the independence of the forenoon. If our Scots tyro say at Westminster,

" I came up from Streatham by car," he will be
supposed to be lord of a magneto, though he came
by the municipal automobile which he must learn
to call a tram.

On inquiring at a house agent concerning a
dwelling he will be asked, " How many reception-
rooms do you wish? " To a Scot who has always
spoken of " public rooms " the London phrase
suggests vast saloons and vistas. Should he ask
" the upset price " of a house that is for sale, the
agent will be upset, and have to admit ignorance of
the connotation of the phrase. It is an odd variation
that English houses are advertised " To be let,"
while Scots houses are announced " To let." The
Scots usage assists the Scots teacher in explaining
the mystery of the gerundial infinitive. The English
phrase gave occasion for the repartee of the attractive young woman who was showing a house in
Sydenham to a possible tenant. With metropolitan
impertinence he said to her, " And are you to be
let along with the house? " " No, sir," she retorted,
" I am to be let alone."

Scottish readers of Dickens are surprised when
Ruth Pinch makes a pudding in a basin, since
Scots housewives use a bowl. In the speech of
Hackney and Kennington and the vocabulary of
Kentish Town and Chiswick, a bowl is bigger than
a basin. Thus while Morningside passes the sugar-
bowl, Clapham passes the sugar-basin. The door-
knocker plays a large part in the stories of Dickens,
as it still does in London suburban houses. Bells
are esteemed a commercial appendage, for offices
have bells, and the Londoner has a knocker on the
front-door, though he may have a bell also. The
knocker has its own ritual. There is the post-
man's knock, which is *sui generis*; there is the caller's
knock, a resonant tattoo; there is the hawker's
knock, a gentle supplication which merely lifts the

clapper and lets it fall. The meaning of a white
kid-glove on a knocker is hid from even marital
eyes in Scotland, an ignorance which would have
disappointed Mr Kenwigs.

Many *English* English household words have to
be learned by the immigrant Scot. He will be
puzzled to find the word "the gutters" exalted
to denote what he called in Edinburgh "the rhones."
He will not obtain a water-barrel for his garden
unless he ask for a cask. He will stare at the door-
handle set in the middle of the door and be surprised when he is asked to "come into the hall"
to find that he enters what he would call a rather
cramped lobby. He will be asked to go round the
garden, for that is the English equivalent to the
Scottish showing of the family album. If he notices
that the fence, which he must not call a paling, is
in need of repair, he must not suggest that a tradesman should mend it. "Tradesman," which means
"craftsman" in Scotland, means in London homes
the butcher, the baker, the grocer.

A Scots week-end guest in a Purley house agreed
readily to accompany his host "to the church,"
which his hostess corrected to "to church." On
setting out he found himself without gloves. "I
left them on the drawers-head in my bedroom,"
said he, and was surprised at the merriment of his
friends that a chest of drawers should be supposed
to have a head. The Scottish love of personification
makes us speak of "head of the road," while London
says, "end of the road"—such anatonomsia is not
practised within sound of Bow Bells. The Scot abroad
in Middlesex or Surrey or on the green plains of
pleasant Hertfordshire may feel his heart leap up
as he beholds the daisies. He will remember that
Burns "pu'd the gowans fine." But he must not
speak of pulling a rose on the banks of Thames,
however often he may have "pu'd a rose" on the

braes of " bonnie Doon." " You Scots are a
ferocious race," an English lady once said to me,
" you speak of pulling flowers; you make me think
of Attila and of the Gauls in Rome." An Englishman picks or plucks flowers. This diversity of usage
excuses somewhat the ignorance of Mr Micawber,
who knew those words of " the immortal exciseman
nurtured beyond the Tweed," but thought that
" gowans " was some sort of beverage at which he
professed his readiness to take a pull. It is safer
also to keep " fine " for linen, wines, china, or to
use it in the sense of delicacy of workmanship,
rather than as a synonym for beautiful. When a
Brixton lady showed a young Scot some pieces of
Breton pottery, he commented, " They are very
fine." " No," said she, " but they are beautiful,
although they are rather coarse. One does not
expect Sevres at St Servan." Whereat the Scot was
much mystified.

Phrases also have their variations, although they
differ more by regions than by nations. The
Glasgow formula of hospitable inquiry at the tea-
table, " Is your tea out? " sounds odd to an Edinburgh hostess, who is accustomed to say with
eastern directness, " Is your cup empty? " Their
London sister says, with the rising inflexion, " A
little more tea, Mrs Nemo? " The canniness of the
one nation and the precipitancy of the other may
be read into the variations.

We have in Lothian a good word for a tiller of
the soil, " hind." Chaucer knew the word as " hine,"
and tells of how the reeve guided him as the Lothian
" grieve " supervises the hinds. The word is
frequent in ballads, as in *Hynd Ettin*. It is a truly
honorific term, meaning originally one who dwelt
" en famille " with the farmer, its Latin synonym
being " familiaris." When, however, a Scots
member of Parliament, addressing the House of

Commons in a debate on agriculture, spoke of
"hinds," an English member, who knew of "hinds"
only as beasts of the chase, protested resentfully
against the use of the word, and asked how the
Scots member would like to be called a "stag."

Probably the linguistic oddity which most sur-
prises a Scot visiting or inhabiting London at the
present time is the apparent supersession of "Yes"
by "That's right." Parliament still maintains its
polysyllabic periphrasis, "The answer is in the
affirmative." In tubes and buses and in the speech
of the man in the street and Gilbert's twopenny-bus
young man "That's right" rules, with an occasional
regency of "Right O!"

"Yes" was once itself a proud usurper, having
been devised to take the place of "yea" when that
earlier affirmative seemed in danger of becoming
"un roi faineant." "Yea" has regained emphasis
in its banishment and from the loyalty of the
Quakers. So the Stewarts in exile and in story have
won love from those who would have opposed them
on the throne. If this new vocable of assent, "That's
right," succeeds in extruding from London speech
time-honoured "Yes," there will be an interesting
parallel to the development of the affirmatives
which gave name to *la langue d'oc* and *la langue d'oil*.

The purpose of speech, except at elections, is
communication of thought. It is well, therefore,
for a transplanted Scot to be linguistically pliable,
not to flaunt his patavinity nor brandish the thistle
unnecessarily. It were not pliancy, however, but
obsequiousness, and even *lèse-majesté* to that robust
letter "r," if a Scot anywhere were to accept the
dicta of certain southern phoneticians and versifiers
that "war" and "saw" are rhymes, and that
"dawning" and "morning" differ in pronunciation only at the initial letter. A Scot who should err
thus would merit Salisbury Crags as a Tarpeian

Rock, or would deserve to be afflicted with the sores of Lazarus or to be dissevered, as were those for whom we shudder as we read in Scripture that they were sawn asunder. These alternatives of penalty would not be distinguishable by the *English* Englishman, who pronounces "saws" and "sores" alike. But Scots were born for higher things, and, if one may say it without arrogance, for a finer discrimination.

Reason and Reasons

IT is not easy in these days to respect the race of men. To describe man as a rational creature is an aspiration, or an outflow of irony, rather than an assertion of obvious fact. Reason herself no longer inspires unanimous reverence. Many declare her a mere Maiden Aunt of mankind, with a barren sceptre in her grasp, clutching, like Queen Victoria, at an authority she cannot justify. It is true that, like Sir Andrew Aguecheek, she was adored once. She must look back regretfully on that golden age when her worshippers, from Hume and Godwin to the Mills and Herbert Spencer, and from Condorcet and D'Alembert to Comte and Taine, vowed to love her till a' the seas of credulity should gang dry and the rocks of prejudice melt wi' the sun of her dialectic. How are the logicians fallen and the weapons of rationalism perished! Under the bludgeonings of the philosophers, from Bergson to Earl Balfour, Reason's head is bloody and low-bowed. Locke, soaring high, set about inquiring concerning human understanding, but the consciousness of human irrationalism restricts modern psychologists to the description of behaviourism. The mighty army of mystics, spiritualists, pragmatists, intuitionalists, roll daily to heaven their pæans of victory over rationalism, and proclaim exultantly the folly of seeking to render a reason. Psycho-analysts and folklorists unite in declaring, "On earth there is nothing so irrational as man: in man there is nothing so unreliable as mind." Who shall honour personality if it be but a congeries of complexes, intertwining and struggling like the worms in a laddie's basket when he goes a-fishing? Who can reverence character if what we call our motives are but a protective coloration of our desires, as the stripes of a tiger in the jungle? Who may label any impulse as heroic, or any activity as ethical, if the highest outrushes of our nature, " the soul that rises with us, our life's star," be, as psycho-analysts maintain, the ebullition of man's discontent that he may not annul the restrictions of affinity, as Moses broke the tables of The Law? Shakespeare may assure us that man is in apprehension how like a god, but they did not know everything down in the Mermaid Tavern! Lord Avebury proved to our fathers that man was a social bungler and a political muddler compared with the ant. M. Fabre in his tireless labours and serried volumes bids us go to the insects and despair of our sluggishness and stupidity as compared with their foresight, sagacity, skill, endurance, determination and zeal. So did King Solomon display to the Queen of Sheba his marvels of wisdom and of art, and put that Research Student in her place as an envious applauder of inimitable wonders. If there be any spirit left in us of self-admiration, Sir J. G. Frazer will cast the sixteen volumes of *The Golden Bough* upon us and destroy the last trace of self-gratulation, as the Sabine invaders cast their shields on the Roman traitress. In Frazer's fascinating but disturbing volumes he who plods may read how man, in his struggle with a Nature, often malignant, always deceitful, but mainly indifferent, has shackled and burdened and fettered himself with reasonless terrors and baseless superstitions and revolting delusions. Ceaselessly the record runs how man has entangled himself, like the ram on Mount Moriah, in thickets of mummery and labyrinths of ritual, persistently absurd and unfailingly ineffective, and has sought to choke his struggling intelligence in swamps of totemistic symbolism and fetid quagmires of magic. One understands why Walt Whitman admired the cows who " do not lie awake in the night groaning over their sins," and why Blake praised the fearful symmetry of the tiger, red in tooth and claw, who undiverted by phantasms or animistic scruples tears his prey in the forests of the night. Even when man came to dwell in communities, half of his intelligence was squandered in inventing methods of defeating or perverting his intelligence. Social life afforded him more occasions, and more varied and poignant means, of torturing himself and his fellows by tabus and terrors, by rites and customs, by mutilations and perversions and restraints. More and more obscuring did he make the veil of sorcery and fear and error with which he swathed his eyes as he looked at the heavens or the world or himself. While we marvel at man's superstition, we must give tribute of admiration to his bravery. Surely " robur et æs triplex " were around his breast who indomitably maintained the will to live, and desire to make live, in face of a hostile Nature which he had reinforced against himself by the phantasmagoria he had devised.

From this gloomy survey of man's story, through which I kept muttering the words of Isaiah, " It is not in man to direct his ways," I was diverted by the shout of one of a pair of boys who had been sounding the hooter of an automobile, temporarily derelict by the side-walk. " Look out! there's the shover " was the slogan that recalled me from pessimism. Those who see in " shover " a mere solecism for " chauffeur " may wonder how I found comfort therein. " Call you these bare events? " said Cromwell, when his critics did not see in certain incidents the expression of God's approval of his policy. " Call you shover a mere error? " say

I. " It is a proof of man's immitigable ardour for reason and of the invulnerability of human intelligence." The heathen of intuitionalism may rage, and the princes of mysticism take counsel together to cast the bonds of reason from them, yet all the ocean of human credulity cannot wash out the tincture of reason from the mind of man. Like a particle of radium in a hill of slag, reason has force within it to move mountains of needless conventions and false belief. Man believes that the world is rational after all. He is convinced that words are not devices for concealing thought. In this faith he will transform a word to make it self-explanatory. The inscrutable " chauffeur " becoming " shover " is the result of the same impulse as stirred in the breast of Galileo as he muttered, " E pur se muove."

It is not only in laboratories, nor yet only in scientific hypotheses, that one sees the effort to invade the frontiers of darkness and extend the diffusion of light. There are many blundering collaborators with the researcher, and yet the light that leads them astray is light from the heaven of reason. When the Hampshire peasant explains that partridges which love to lie in the furrows are so named because they " part the ridges," he is brother of Littré under the skin. So the Yorkshire woman assured Wordsworth that Greta was named from its bridge which " you can see is just a great A." A Londoner speaks of donning his mackintosh, but the Essex farmer, who never heard of Moy Hall or the son of the " toisich," speaks of putting on his " mucking togs " for dirty weather. In *The Bride of Lammermoor*, Sir Walter tells of the baking of " carcakes, cookies, and petticoat-tails." The last is a reckless adventure to rationalize to a Scottish ear " petits gatels," small cakes of a French fashion. Slogan is Gaelic " sluagh gairm," and means " battle cry." Gavin Douglas, whose own surname remembers the language of Alban, and who might have learned good Gaelic spelling at Dunkeld, makes the word in his *Æneid*, "slugh orne," which others printed "slughorn." Robert Browning, confusing the call to battle with the instrument of summons, thought "slughorn" was some kind of bugle, and wrote in *Childe Roland to the Dark Tower came*—"Dauntless the slughorn to his lips he set." Examples of this popular rationalizing or folk-etymology are numerous. The Scot still knows that a horse may "reist," and that a man too may turn "reisty," or intractable and obstinate. But the Englishman has lost the old word and has made the phrase into "turn rusty," as if it were a metaphor from the slow movement of a rusty key. The word "female" should be "femel," as it is in *Piers Plowman*, being from French "femelle," a diminutive from Latin "femina." It has no etymological relation with "male." To keep woman in her place of subordination and bear witness to her dependence on the male, "femel" was changed into "female." The old spelling should be restored, in accordance with The Sex Disabilities Removal Act. When will some ardent feminist press for the removal also of the innuendo in the spelling of wo-man, that perversion of wif-man? The change, no doubt, was devised by some mediæval celibate when admonishing the daughters of Eve for their responsibility for all our woe, and loss of Eden.

In *Macbeth*, Lennox tells the Thane of Cawdor that "the obscure bird clamoured the livelong night." It is natural to suppose that livelong is "long living," but "live" is in truth a corruption of "lief" (dear) as in "leman" (leofman) of the ballads. The expression "livelong night" belongs to the same class as the modern "the whole blessed night." Those who go to Dunfermline to revere the grave of The Bruce will see the ruins of the Fratery.

With that dangerous thing, a little knowledge of Latin, they will explain the word as the hall of the "fratres." Yet "fratery" is but a doublet of "refectory." *Piers Plowman* speaks of "Freres in here freitour," and Langland's word is from French *refretoir*, from Low Latin *refectorium*.

Place-names have given wide scope to the pseudo-rationalizing of the folk-etymologist. Every region of Scotland has its absurd explanations of local names. Everyone knows the explanation of Holyrood as deriving from the legend of the cross which appeared between the antlers of the stag which King David was hunting near Arthur's Seat. The legend is really derived from the name, and is common to many countries. The name of the Abbey in the foundation charter, "Ecclesia Crucis," is a monkish gloss on the name, like naming the Abbey of Glenluce, "Ecclesia Vallis Lucis," or "Mons Rosarum" for Monross (Montrose). If Holyrood is to be explained in the language of Duncan Bhan, it may be "choille ruigh," slope of the hill, a precise description of its situation. It might also be "choille ruadh," the red hill. To this day the hill of bare screes among its emerald turf gleams like rubies.

Most of the names in the valley of the Lothian Esk are Celtic (Brythonic or Gaelic) and have the Celtic euphony, Penicuik, Auchendinny, Roslin, Lasswade, Kevock, Dalkeith, Melvin — spoiled to Melville — Pittendreigh, Lasswade, where Scott wrote several of his early poems, and where Drummond of Hawthornden lies, as he wished, "Where roses shade the place," is a difficult name to explain. Chalmers invented words which he called Anglo-Saxon to compass a derivation. The form Lochswaid appears on an old tombstone and Laghswad in the Darien Papers. The word is locally divided in pronunciation as La-swade, as if in compensation for the lost guttural. The first syllable is probably "lagh," a hollow, and if "wade" be taken as "Bhaid," from "baad," a wood, the "s" may represent some connective. The meaning would thus be "the hollow by the wood," or "the woody hollow," a precise description of the early appearance of the place.

If, however, you ask the village children the meaning of the name, they will tell you one of the most absurd examples of folk-etymology that ignorance, or perhaps humour, ever devised. Here is the local derivation, set in rhyme by some wag, and to be purchased on postcards.

> When there was nae brig to cross the Esk river,
> On Jenny's braid back they a' gaed thegither.
> For Jenny was sober and honest and steady.
> She carried the laird, she carried his leddy.
> When the laird he was mounted, the doggie first gaed.
> Syne waving his stick he cried, " Jenny, lass, wade!"

Who reasons awry, is yet Reason's disciple. Folk-etymology, for all its absurdities, is a proof that man, though he may be frighted with false fire and go astray after many a will-o'-the-wisp, has his face towards the light.

Virgilian Echoes ✑   ✑   ✑

SOME scholars deny to Virgil the authorship of
the *Culex*, and refuse to believe that the poet of
Juno's wrath and Dido's woes lamented the fate
of a gnat. Yet the tale of the kindly insect killed by
the unwitting shepherd whom he had saved from
death has, in a special degree, the Virgilian sense of
" lacrimæ rerum." As Allan Ramsay reminds us:
" Ere bairns can read, they first maun spell "; and
Virgil may well have tried his prentice hand on
the *Culex* before he sang of wars and rural life and
pious heroes. Edmund Spenser accepted the poem
as Virgil's, and translated it in many charming
stanzas of *ottava rima*. I wonder if any Scots teacher
of the classics has ever studied with his class the
Culex and Spenser's version side by side? Teachers
are as timorous about frontiers as Foreign Office
officials. I wish they would cross the " march
dykes " of their subject more often, and even, on
fit occasion, be owre the border an' awa. One can
always camouflage such a raid as correlation.

Classical students who love the rigour of the
critical game, and who neither accept the plea
" lusimus," nor yield to the appeal " doctrina,
vaces licet," should consult an article on the *Culex*
in *Classical Philology*, vol. v., by Professor Phillimore.
If anyone " impar congressus Achilli " thereafter
remains unconvinced, " pondere vel culicis levior
famaque feretur."

Gavin Douglas's translation of the *Æneid* is a
bright rose in the chaplet of Scottish literature. He
has had few followers. Has some dread of the *sortes*

Virgilianæ deterred others from treading in Gavin's footsteps? There are various passages in the *Georgics* which cry aloud and shout for the favour of the Doric muse. That accomplished translator and true poet, Mr J. Logie Robertson, has shown how the wisdom and camaraderie of Horace are suited to our homespun speech. Some of his own pastorals and idyls are worthy of the poet of the *Eclogues* and of his teacher Theocritus. The Sicilian poet would have allowed him the praise Milon gives to Bucæus, ὡς εὖ τὰν ἰδέαν τᾶς ἁρμονίας ἐμέτρησεν, but would have rallied him on greeting Queen Cypris only from afar, like Hippolytus. "Hugh Halliburton" is perhaps of the mind of Æschinas, that there is but a hairbreadth between the lover and the madman.

The following verses are suggested by the passage in the *Culex*, "O bona pastoria," but they wander widely from the text. Their background is the Moorfoot hills—a pastoral range which "caret vate sacro."

THE SHEPHERD OF THE MOORFOOTS

I wadna leave the shepherd's life upon the braes o' Muirfit
To be an Indian king that sees his slaves come loutin barefit.
The Muirfits hae nae fleechin ways, but glumshin, gurly weather,
Auld scrunts o' birk that sough an' skraigh, an' anterin clumps o'
*   heather ;*
The snell wind meets ye up the hopes tho' spring is saft in Lowden,
An' mony a day, near the hint o' May, flauchans o' snaw come
*   crowdin ;*
But aye the air blaws caller there, nae claiks nor clash can deave ye
Unless the whaups or, frae the fanks, the wheengin gimmers grieve
*   ye ;*
Ye hae the warld a' to yoursel, the firmament owrehangs ye,
Ye micht be Adam ere Eve cam, an' a' life's collieshangie ;
The warld below plays oot its play in steadin, loan, or burgh :
Yonder's a gabbart near The May, an' there's the plooman's
*   furrow,*
An' yon's the reek frae Embro toon whaur folk at mart or session
Are raxin eager efter gear, on ithers' cuits aye pressin.

Wad they but speel the braes wi' me an' learn the joys they're
    tynin.
What tho' wi' gowd the spleuchan swell if aye the soul be dwinin?
For bruckle ware, baith late an' ear', body an' mind to trauchle
Gars mony a life that ettled fair end worthless as a bauchle ;
Ye micht as weel wi' winlestraes frae Blaik'ope mak a tether,
Or seek by Garvald Sykes at Yule the crimson flush o' heather,
As thirl yoursel to serve for things sae frush as fame or siller,
Girst stored in geisened girnals buiks gey sma' afore the miller.
He kens the lownest neuk in life that lets the warld gae by him,
Content to dae his darg an' see cuifs thrive, yet ne'er envy them.
It isna here we should seek gear, we're bid " abune to lay it,"
The lowsin-time's near-han' for a', an' nae man can delay it.
The brier that blooms at Beltane fades ere Lammas has owreta'en
    it,
Our life flits by as fast, an' yet we're sweir to learn to hain it.
Hope draws us here, fear drives us there, this dream, syne that, we
    lippen,
Afore we ken we're near the end an' Time is frae us slippin.
The years gae rinnin as the burns brattle withoot devallin
Till hirplin carles wi' pows like snaw succeed the stirrin callan ;
The Leithen bickers to the Tweed, the Heriot seeks the Gala,
The Tyne snooves eastward its ain' gait by Crichton an' yont Fala,
But syne or sune they a' win hame, like the hirsel at the gloamin,
An' a' are happit owre to sleep aneth the ocean's foamin.

Misnomers ✑   ✑   ✑   ✑

IN the Middle Ward of Clydesdale, in the parish of Libberton, there is a craggy knoll where in old days the hawk nested. It was known as Gledstanes, the rocky home of the hawk or gled, and its lairds were Gledstanes of that ilk, as their thrughstanes by Biggar Kirk bear witness to this day. In 1296 a Herbert de Gledstan did homage to Edward I. of England, and a Herbert Glaidstanes was made a bailie of Dundee in 1562. The bailie's son, George Glaidstanes, became in 1604 Archbishop of St Andrews, and is reviled with ugly epitaphs in Row's *History of the Kirk of Scotland*. I wish that a gled had pykit oot the e'en of him who first changed the meaningful name of Gledstane to the meaningless Gladstone. Those who remember the greatest of the name, and who recall the craggy brow, the eagle profile, and the hawk-like eye, or who have watched as he launched into a peroration, like some great bird with curve of wing sweeping through the air in effortless involution, will agree that Gledstane was the fitter name, and will regret that our forefathers mangled it.

This is but one instance of that Scottish weakness which " ca's a schule an academy," and changes significant Scots names into pretentious English impostures. The fisher folk of East Lothian still speak of Aberleddy, which is probably Celtic for " the broad slope," but ignorance has turned " leddy " into " lady," and one must soil the lips with Aberlady when desiring a railway ticket thither. I would " stick them a' in Aberleddy " and elsewhere, who thus remove the ancient land-marks of nomenclature.

The leprosy has spread widely. Lann-niddry has been anglicized into Longniddry, although the village is as short as a dirk, and Gledsmuir, the moor of the hawk, has become Gladsmuir, with the second syllable pronounced to rhyme with " sure," though it should be said to rhyme with " sair." Who has not felt that Musselburgh is a ridiculous name for a town of historic significance and of charming aspect? If the name is written as in the thirteenth century, Muschelburh, it will start other spirits. For Muschel may be " Mas Choille," Celtic for " the bare hill." In all Lothian there is no height so important as that on which the church of Inveresk has succeeded a primeval fort which commanded the crossing of the Esk, and bridled all who sought to assail Edinburgh from the south. Muschel was the fort; Muschelburgh the town which grew up by the fort and later by the bridge which the fort controlled. But all that is lost in Musselburgh.

There is a parish in Nithsdale named nowadays Irongray, which mingles memories of A. K. H. B. with thoughts of Helen Walker, whose story gave Scott the idea of Jeanie Deans' journey to London. No one calls it Irongray except post-office folks, and school people, and Presbytery clerks. It is Airngray, a name that would adorn a sonnet, being probably Celtic for " the height on the moor." But someone who thought he was speaking delicately changed " Airn " into " Iron " in the folly of a little knowledge. If there is a Scots name with more romance around it than Douglas has, I know it not. Yet the name of him " who was in al his deedis leal " has lost a rose from its chaplet since men have said its first syllable to rhyme with " bug." The wonderful refrain in *The Buke of the Howlet,*

" O Douglas! O Douglas! tender and true " is an archangel damaged if one does not make the " ou " sound as in French, and thus foreshadow the same wooing note in " true."

All over Scotland this plague of perversion meets one. Decent Kinedart masquerades as King Edward; Kingorm, the blue headland, is spoiled into Kinghorn; Balmerino, where Queen Ermyngarde sleeps in the ruined abbey, is accented by the ignorant not on the ante-penult but on the penult, as if the merino sheep pastured on its bonnie braes. Place-names and personal names alike have been debased and obscured. Early in the eighteenth century there dwelt in Menteith a cow-feeding family named Neilson, descendants of some Neil of the Gregarach who had abjured his royal name in its time of prescription. Oddly enough, the Neilsons were Cameronians or MacMillanites, and walked eight miles each Sabbath to their kirk in the Craigs of Stirling. One of the Neilsons ventured to Edinburgh, opened a shop at the head of the West Bow, and sold Bibles and Catechisms to country folk descending the sanctified bends o' the Bow to the Grassmarket. When the firm began to trade with England in the days of Nelson's glory at the Nile and Trafalgar, worthy Mr Neilson found English booksellers and bankers writing his name as Nelson. He dropped the " i " from his name, to the grave discontent of some of his kin at Kippen, which is " oot o' the warld " and sees no reason for compromises. To their expostulations he made the witty rejoinder, " I am like the great Admiral Nelson; I have lost an 'i' in the service of my country." But there is neither such wit nor any wisdom in the " malfaitours " who deface our Scottish names. The red plague rid them for marring thus our language!

L

Christian Names ✑ ✑ ✑

Scots Tradition

" KEEP oot o' the dubs, Conrad, ye're fylin your guid shoon."

I heard a Scots mother the other day thus address her boy, who was dipping his shoes in the puddles of the rain-swept street. The name set me musing how Scottish usage has changed with regard to Christian names. Conrad for a Scots boy! Was it from Joseph Conrad, or from Conrad Montfichet?

Scots tradition used to require that the first boy should be named after the father's father, the second after the mother's father; after which the names of uncles, firstly paternal, then maternal, were invoked. To give a boy a Christian name from whim or for its euphony would have branded him as a kinless loon, or as having forbears whose names were better forgotten. "Nous avons changé tout cela," and parents name their children in accordance with the rule of the Abbey of Thelema, " Fay ce que tu vouldras."

A Christian name, the name given at baptism, was, in the beginning at least, chosen from the Scriptures or from the records of the saints. The usage still prevails for those who live " in religion." It led, especially in France, to a multiplicity of names, as parents wished to have their children under the protection of several saints. Marshal MacDonald, in addition to the name of Alexander, which he owed to his Scots ancestry, was Joseph, James and Stephen. The practice led to boys being

given the names of women saints: thus Stevenson's
Viscount St Ives was named Anne, a saint to whom
Brittany pays a high devotion. In reaction against
these names of saints the supporters of the French
Revolution selected front-names for their children
from the heroes of the Greek and Roman republics.
Thus Aristide—the front-name of the late M. Briand
—Hippolyte, Julien, Epaminondas, César, Valère
are not infrequent still in France.

English Puritans chose names for their children
from the Bible, especially from the Old Testament.
The usage has continued in Dissenting circles,
and Jesse, Obed, Caleb, Seth are not uncommon
in England. Extremists even burdened a child
with a phrase as a Christian name. Barbon, an
Anabaptist member of Cromwell's Little Parliament,
had " Praise-God " as his Christian name. Persons
of scanty humour thought it a jest to pervert his
surname to Barebone. Ben Jonson, in his play
Bartholomew Fair, names characters Zeal-of-the-Land
Busy and Win-the-Fight Littlewit, but Ben is not
good evidence for the prevalence of such absurdities
outside a satirical play. I once found a girl in an
English school laden with the Christian name
Kerenhappuch, the name of one of the daughters
of Job. One was relieved to learn that her
companions called her Kernie. And I knew an
older, attractive maiden whose parents had labelled
her Mizpah, which repelled admirers. To say
" Miss Mizpah " daunted most youths, and an
attractive abbreviation of Mizpah was not easily
devised. The man she married said to me, " I just
called her ' Darling ' from the very first." Thus do
the violent take heaven by force.

The giving of Old Testament names to children
has never prevailed in Scotland, though Adam is
fairly common, in spite of the Catechism's insistence
on " the guilt of Adam's first sin." Dr M'Crie,

when scourging Sir Walter Scott for his unhistoric representation of the Covenanters in *Old Mortality*, rightly called attention to the unfairness of giving ministers such grotesque names as Habakkuk Mucklewrath, Peter Poundtext, Ephraim MacBriar, Gabriel Kettledrummle. You will search in vain for parallels to these in the records of the time or in Wodrow, or Patrick Walker, or Howie. The only Scots Habakkuk I have been able to trace was a Habakkuk Bisset, who wrote a legal treatise, *The Rolment of Courtis*, in the early seventeenth century. An English Puritan, whose son was born in the year of the Restoration, was so moved by the downfall of the Commonwealth that he named the child Ichabod. As Ichabod Dawks he became a noted author of news-letters and an important figure in the history of journalism.

Behind all such purposive choice lies the hope that the name will have an effect upon the child. Stevenson argues charmingly that he would have been different if he had not borne the same Christian name as Robert le Diable, Robert Fergusson and Robert Burns. Does naming a boy Samuel dispose him to early piety? If you shorten that name to Sam, it is more likely that you will expect from the boy, since Dickens, a wholly secular wit. The strongest believer in the influence of Christian names whom I have known was a citizen of Birmingham who named one of his sons Martin Luther and the other Isaac Newton. Martin became a worthy mayor of a notable English borough, but Isaac Newton died in youth, borne down by his names.

In Scottish usage there are certain front-names which "go with" certain surnames. Alan goes with Stewart, Torquil with MacLeod, Sholto with Douglas, Hector (Gaelic Eachin) with MacDonald, Parlane with MacFarlane, Hew (so spelled) with Dalrymple, etc. Those are unlucky who have a front-name which is epicene, either in sound or spelling, as Evelyn, Francis, Frances. The works of Evelyn Waugh have been more than once assigned to a woman novelist.

It is natural that girls should be given the names of flowers, Rose, Lily, Violet; but the preference for Ivy, which is strong in some parts of England, is puzzling. When first I read Meredith's *Rhoda Fleming* I found it not easy to give any sympathy to Dahlia. That was in the time of the early dahlias, showy in colour, but rigid in form, like wax-flowers come to life.

Some men, and more women, have ventured to change their Christian names. The most noted of these was perhaps that strange personality of the French Revolution, Baron Jean Baptiste de Clootz, later known as Anacharsis Clootz. Carlyle writes of him " dropping baptisms and feudalisms . . . he wandered over this terraqueous planet seeking, one may say, the paradise we lost long ago." When there is much talk now about the world-state, it might be worth while for someone to reopen his once-famous *Base Constitutionelle de la République du Genre Humaine*. He assumed his odd front-name from the Abbé Barthélemy's book, *Voyage du jeune Anacharsis*, the fictitious journey of a young Scythian to the Greek republics in the fourth century B.C.

Parallels   ❦   ❦   ❦   ❦

BEFORE football had reached its modern autocracy, in which it bears no brother near its throne, as Pope said of Addison and the Sultan, there was a game in Scottish playgrounds called Cuddieloup, a development of leapfrog. One boy stood against a wall, another boy curved his spine, and placed his head on the stomach of the first; two or three others, similarly arching their bodies, attached themselves in sequence to the rear of the second. Then one other boy with a flying leap would get astride his earth-regarding comrades. who would curvet and prance to dislodge him, If, however, the incubus, clinging though titubating, could reach without mishap the back of the first of line, the second act of the game began. Seated like Don Quixote on Rosinante, this protagonist would raise in air so many fingers, and chant, " Back! Back! hoo mony fingers do I haud up? " If his bearer guessed aright the boy by the wall would intone, " Three you say, and three there are. Back! Back! stand up! " Thereupon the successful guesser became the next onleaper; the linkage moved forward, and the cavalier became last of line. If the guess went awry, the test was renewed until a correct surmise was made. As the game is played in the North of England, the formula of inquiry is, " Buck! Buck! how many horns do I hold up? "

What is essentially the same game is referred to in the *Satyricon of Petronius*. I am not to be held as

recommending anyone to read that work of the
" Arbiter Elegantiarum," the dissolute companion
of Nero, yet " qualis artifex " in Latin prose.
Rather would I advise that whoever reads it should
follow the injunction of Leviticus—" bathe himself
in water and be unclean until the even." For only
La Garçonne exceeds it in shamelessness. Trimalchio,
the chief character in the *Satyricon*, bids his favourite
Crœsus leap on his back. The boy at once " usus
est equo." The phrase would be best translated
by the words in which David Lyndsay tells James V.
" as a pedlar bears his pack, I bore thee stridelings
on my back." Then Crœsus clapped Trimalchio
on the shoulders and, holding up his fingers, said,
" Bucca! Bucca! quot sunt hic? "—*i.e.* how many
are there? cheek, cheek! Probably the cheek of
the bearer was tapped with one hand while the
other extended the fingers. The Apostle Paul, as
he went about Rome, laden with his chains, may
have seen the game and heard the call, " Bucca!
bucca! " English boys have pseudo-rationalized
the word into " Buck! " and have substituted
" horns " for " fingers." Whether the legends of
Robin Hood have anything to do with the change
or whether there is an innuendo of " wearing the
horn " were to inquire too curiously. The Scots
schoolboy has changed " Bucca! " into " Back! "
which is rather meaningless, but he has kept the
" fingers." It were easy to suggest that the game
may derive from rites of initiation and to see in
this sport of boys the debris of ancient mysteries.

I do not know if any student of genetic psychology
has ever suggested that a baby gets its first ideas of
externality from its fingers. Certainly children are
very interested in the differences of the fingers, and
they enjoy the rhymes which discriminate their
fortunes. The Scots rhyme, which begins with the
thumb, is such as one would expect to survive from

the time when the key could not keep the castle
or the barn, nor the bracken bush, the cow:

> *This is the man that broke the barn;*
> *This is the man that stole the corn;*
> *This is the man that sell't a';*
> *This is the man that tell't a';*
> *And wee pirlie-winkie got the blame o' a'.*

The French parallel is rustic and less law-breaking,
but it also laments the lot of the little finger:

> *Celui-ci a vu le lièvre;*
> *Celui-ci l'a couru;*
> *Celui-ci l'a tenu;*
> *Celui-ci l'a mangé;*
> *Celui-ci n'a rien eu,*
> *Il a dit à sa mère,*
> *Je n'ai pas eu, je n'ai pas eu.*

Many nursery rhymes are also riddles, as in Humpty
Dumpty. The French parallel in an archaic form is:

> *Boule, boule, sur le keyere:*
> *Boule, boule, par terre:*
> *Y n'a nuz homme en Angleterre;*
> *Pou l'erfaire.*

I take " keyere " to be for " chœur," here used as
for wall of the church. The English rhyme has the
advantage of a quaint yet exactly descriptive name
for the egg. It is also more poetic, since " all the
king's horses and all the king's men " has all the
age of chivalry echoing through it. Our Scots
rhyme for " riding " a child upon the knee seems
more appropriate to the different speeds than any
of its parallels:

> *This is the way the ladies ride,*
> *Jimp and sma',*
> *Jimp and sma';*
> *This is the way the gentlemen ride,*
> *Spurs and a',*
> *Spurs and a';*
> *This is the way the cadgers ride,*
> *Creels and a',*
> *Creels and a'!*

The breakneck riding of the cadger with an empty creel, all goods sold, hoofs pounding and creels bumping, is the climax of delight to a child. That delight should have been at least noticed in Stevenson's *Garden of Verses*. But on consideration it may be argued that the poems in that book are mainly about the play of a sedentary only child, not a stirrin' loon or ramstam wean. The rhyme may be used by teachers to remind pupils how late it was before goods could be conveyed in many parts of Scotland by wheel-traffic, and how important pack-horses and cadgers with their creels were. Scott was accurate as usual when he painted that fine scene in *Guy Mannering* of the gipsies leaving Ellangowan with their cuddies and their creels, and Godfrey Bertram surveying them with regret and a twinge of remorse as he listened to the valedictory of Meg Merrilees.

The German parallel is, " So reiten die Herren. . . . So reiten die Bauern. . . . So reiten die Husaren." The contrasts are not discriminated so effectively as in the Scots rhyme. The French rhyme, " Sur le pont d'Avignon," has a dignity that befits the old Papal city.

Our number rhymes, as " One, two, buckle my shoe, etc.," have something abrupt about them. There is little continuity of thought; they seem to have been framed for a time when the intellect was short-winded. The corresponding French rhyme has in contrast a connecting thread :

> *Un, deux, trois; j'irai dans le bois:*
> *Quatre, cinq, six; chercher les cerises;*
> *Sept, huit, neuf; dans mon panier neuf;*
> *Dix, onze, douze; elles seront tout rouges.*

It is worth while noting the advantage French has in being able to rhyme neuf (new) with neuf (nine), a liberty forbidden in English, in which no versifier would escape censure if he rhymed " dew " with

" due " or " knew " with " new." Chaucer used a wider freedom, since in the *The Prologue to the Canterbury Tales* he wrote: " The holy blisful martyr for to seeke That hem hath holpen when that they were seeke." Perhaps it was well to make the hurdles higher in our language of facile rhymes.

Mickle and Muckle ✑   ✑   ☞

DR BALLARD, in his wise and witty book,
The New Examiner, heads a chapter " Mickle
and Muckle." Dr Ballard has scholarship enough
in English, as in so much else, to know that there
is something wrong with the heading. He therefore
appends a note: " Etymologically the words
' Mickle ' and ' Muckle ' are identical in meaning;
but they are here used in the popular sense to which
currency has been given by the proverb, ' Many a
mickle makes a muckle.' " It is sadly true that
many English people think there is such a proverb,
but it is a pity that Dr Ballard, having put his hand
to the plough of investigation, should have turned
back so soon. It is gratifying to us Scots that the
English should borrow our proverbs to supplement
their scanty store, but they should not deform them.
They can take their choice of the proverb in the
form, " Mony a pickle maks a mickle," or in the
form, " Mony a puckle maks a muckle." If they
find these unintelligible they should content themselves with " Many littles make much," or, like
Silas Wegg, drop into poetry, and say:

> *Little drops of water,*
>   *Little grains of sand,*
> *Make the mighty ocean*
>   *And the solid land.*

It is hard, however, to overtake an error which
has got a start. Years ago the same malformation
of the proverb appeared in one of those ingenious
advertisements, " The Opinions of Callisthenes,"
with which Mr Selfridge instructed and allured the

Londoner. I called his attention to the mistake, and he had the correction issued with the same publicity. But the error is still running.

It is interesting to speculate what leads to such perversions. The first cause is the risk anyone runs in borrowing from another language. Everyone will recall the grotesque misapplications of French words that prevailed in the War. To say " Mony a mickle maks a muckle " deprives the proverb of the jingle of rhyme, which is one of its appeals. It gives it, however, an alliteration which the Scots form does not show. Is the English alteration then an atavistic sign, the Old English preference for verse on an alliterative basis reasserting itself? Have we here " The Ormulum " stretching its regulative hand gropingly through the centuries?

When English friends say to me, " But which is the correct form, ' Mony a pickle maks a mickle,' or ' Mony a puckle maks a muckle' ? " I answer, " Both." Then I go on to point out that literary Scots has not yet become unified, standardized, formalized like literary English. Scots is still at the stage of English in Chaucer's day, when three forms were almost equipollent. No writer in Scots has had the regulative power which Chaucer had on English. The Scots of Burns and Scott may be taken generally as the form of literary Scots, yet their usage has never had any restrictive power. Burns drew his Scots quite as much from the old Scots writers as from the speech of Carrick or Kyle. Scott's Scots is more definitely regional Scots, naturally so, as mainly prose, and deserves Stevenson's phrase, " The brave metropolitan utterance of Sir Walter." Ilka land has its ain lauch, and why Angus should say, " I'm gaen awa," and Lothian say, " I'm gaun away," and the one say, " I winna ging," while the other says, " I winna gang," is a matter of surmise and not of certainty. One thing is clear however, the Scots poet should not say "ging"; he must use the "gang" form or the "gae" form, unless he seeks a purely regional effect and audience. "Mickle," which may be spelled "meikle," as Dunbar and Burns spell it, though not uniformly, is nearest to the original form. Most of Southern Scotland nowadays says "muckle," and it would be absurd to write of "Mickle-Mou'd Meg." This change from *i* to *u* may become an ugliness, as when Dundonians make "hill" into "hull." Burns always uses, I think, "twa," but much of Southern Scotland says "twae." "Twa" is, as it was in King Alfred's day, the neuter form of the numeral. But "twae" is not therefore erroneous. It is the obliterated form of the masculine numeral "twegen," which passes through "tweyen" to "twain," but occurs also as early as Chaucer as "tweye." In a pathetic passage in *The Knightes Tale* the wounded knight says, "Softe tak me in your armes tweye."

One of the limitations of the English language is that it must use the same word in "a little boy" and "a little money." French can say, "un petit garçon" and "un peu d'argent," and Scots can say "a wee laddie" and "a puckle siller." Scots is indeed felicitous in the variety and the delicacy of its nouns of multitude. The man who can discriminate precisely between "a puckle," "a wheen" and "a curn," and give illustrative examples from speech and literature, is a deacon of the craft of Scots letters. The original meaning of "pickle" is a grain. Burns uses it in that sense in *Hallowe'en* : "Her tap pickle maist was lost." The Catechism of Archbishop Hamilton, who was captured in the assault by the Lords of the Congregation in Dumbarton Castle and hanged at Glasgow, uses the word in a fine sentence which may be cited as an example of good Scots prose, or of Scots euphuism, or of the prelate's zeal for his faith. "As breid is maid of mony pickels of corn and wyne is maid of mony berryis and ane body is maid of mony membris, sa the kirk of God is gadderit togidder within the band of perfit lufe and cheritie and festinit with the spreit of God." In the more fluid prose of the next generation the word occurs again in the *Letters of Samuel Rutherford*, our Scottish Jeremy Taylor, who needed but a pickle more restraint and a pickle less discursiveness to reach at least to the shoulder of the Bishop of Down. "When the last pickle o' sand shall be at the nick o' fallin doon in your hour-glass, ye will esteem the bloom of this world's glory like the colours of the rainbow that no man can put in his purse and treasure." Some unknown songster of the eighteenth century has written a delightful stanza:

> *O gin my love were a pickle o' wheat,*
> *And growing upon yon lily lea,*
> *And I mysel a bonny wee bird,*
> *Awa wi' that pickle I wad flee.*

The Tennysonian lover who longed to be first the necklace and then the girdle of his lady does not so convince of his sincerity as this esurient rural lover.

> *There's a pickle o' fowk say " mickle,"*
> *And a puckle that " muckle " say ;*
> *And a curn o' fowk that aye say " twa,"*
> *And a wheen that aye say " twae."*

> *And some say, " Nannie, will ye gang ? "*
> *And ithers, " Will ye gae ? "*
> *And deave us wi' their clavers*
> *Owre splittin o' a strae.*

> *Wi' jist ae sark to change the ither*
> *A chiel's ill aff and bare ;*
> *That's a gey puir hoose that hasna*
> *Some plenishin to spare.*

> *Oor auld Scots tongue has rowth o' gear,*
> *She keeps nae scrimpit board ;*
> *" Fill fu' and fetch mair," is their cry,*
> *That kens hoo weel she's stored.*

The Chapper-up   ⌀   ⌀   ⌀

THERE are occasions in a Scots winter when even the most patriotic of us are tempted to think that Bannockburn was a mistake and to wish that our forefathers had left Scotland to the invaders and had sought a home in a more genial clime under skies less chill. The temptation assails most strongly those who have to begin their day's darg so early in the morning before the break of day. Faith in the charm of Scotland under a sleety Januar' wind at five A.M. meets the definition in the Epistle to the Hebrews in being " the evidence of things not seen." Oak and triple brass are around his breast who can face without a murmur the transition from his bed's embracing warmth, the struggle of tabetless fingers with the ritual of raiment, the constraining of dozened limbs to front the frost that freezes fell, the venturing under skies that seem irrecoverably dark, without all hope of day, and the sullen aspect of a world that scowls on those who gaze upon her ere she is buskit.

Milton has some pretty lines on the joys of labour " when the dappled dawn doth rise." But Milton was thinking of summer time. In any case, there is not much weight in the evidence of a poet who tells us that " the ploughman whistles o'er the furrowed land " at that season. Poetic praises of morning toil have come most frequently from urban dwellers who have never ventured to sample the pleasures they celebrate, and from book-lovers who are known to sit late and lie correspondingly. Gray, who often did not rise till noon, could know only by hearsay of the rude forefathers "how jocund did they drive their team afield." I find more convincingness and more trace of personal experience in Scott's lines on sunrise in the city:

> *The sun awakening through the smoky air*
> *Of the dark city sends a sullen glance,*
> *Rousin' each caitiff to his task of care,*
> *Of sinful man the sad inheritance.*

I am sure that is an autobiographic touch from an Edinburgh morning of haar when the youthful Scott had to rise early to drive his quill on law papers. Not even an urban poet, however, has ventured to sing of the joys of early rising in winter. The *communis sensus* of Scots toilers is expressed in the old song:

> *Up in the mornin's no' for me,*
> *Up in the mornin' early,*
> *When a' the fields are covered wi' snaw.*

A modern song announces the same feeling, though with less art:

> *It's fine to get up in the mornin'*
> *But it's better to lie in your bed.*

Discouragement to early rising in winter comes not only from external conditions. Wives and mothers know that what is called by a kindly peri-phrasis, "rising on the wrong side," is more frequent about the winter solstice. Voltaire is reported to have said that no one could be expected to be fully civilized before ten A.M. It is a strong proof of the high character of our Scottish ministers that they crowd, during the Assembly week, to Moderator's breakfasts, and gree throughout them. Only at dinners and suppers may normal faulty men be assembled if concord and harmony are to be assured.

In Milton's description of the delights of a summer morning he has the line:

> *And every shepherd tells his tale*
> *Under the hawthorn in the dale.*

The line means that the shepherds count their sheep to see if any have gone amissing in the night. I have known sentimental teachers, editors, and illustrators conceive the line as referring to the love-making of a Corydon or a Thyrsis. Five-o'clock-in-the-morning courage may be the highest type of bravery, but ante-lucan love-making has found no praisers. Neither Catullus nor Robert Burns, those flaming torches of love, nor Theocritus nor Bion, although they dwelt by Sicilian seas, have sung of love before the dawn. Foolish Cloten in *Cymbeline* set his choristers to warble under Imogen's window when the lark at heaven's gate sings, but with no avail. Only Iachimo heard of the chaliced flowers. James Hogg knew better the times and the seasons. He wrote of the shepherd who

> *Downa gae to bed for his heart is in a flame*
> *To meet his bonny lassie when the kye comes hame.*

Burns too recommends " a cannie 'oor at e'en ": and we may credit his expertise.

Men will ever debate whether the former days were better than these. " The young laugh at the past; the auld laugh at the present." Few will deny that modern usage has done well in postponing the summons to toil, especially in winter. One shivers as one remembers that in the Middle Ages children went to school at six o'clock. The same early hour was until recently fixed for the beginning of labour for most workers. Dwellers in a town of mills and factories will recall the raucous or ear-piercing sirens, hooters, whistles which tore the morning gloom and slumber, the dishevelled haste of the somnolent who sallied at the summons, the snuggling satisfaction of those whose hour had not yet come, the hurrying transit under the blae repellent skies, the clatter of feet in the dark streets, and the converging streams of toilers that surged

M

within the mill gates, leaving behind them solitude
and gloom. Some towns had not dared devise such
concordant summons by discords. Many toilers
also feared they might " sleep in," and be in worse
lot than even the foolish virgins in not hearing when
the cry was made. As yet alarm clocks were not.
Sleepyheads and doubters therefore engaged a
herald, a chapper-up, who should wake them with
his knocking. Some weakly youth, unfit for toil,
some sexagenarian, waukrife with rheumatism,
agreed to knock daily, for a consideration, at the
doors or windows of his clientele. The chapper-up
was thus a perambulating tocsin; like Macbeth, he
murdered sleep. He was the macer or bedellu
of labour, the apparitor of the lords of toil, the
doomster of the penalty of Adam. Where "lands"
of tenements rose high, he bore a long pole
telescopic in make, and sent his signal of insistenc
therewith to the upper storeys. This was his wand
of a potency opposed to that of Comus, since tha
compelled inaction, while the chapper-up's ro
said, like Satan's summons in Pandemonium
" Awake, arise! "

" Chap " is a good Scots word, which is rathe
out of use to-day in Southern Scotland, althoug
Angus keeps it going, as Sir James Barrie show
" The knock's chappin'. I jalouse it's gey nea
lowsin' time." Many Scots could not translat
that sentence into English or say it with prope
vocalization. " Chap was often used metaphoricall
by preachers to describe the voice of conscienc
Zachary Boyd, for instance, laments regarding a
offender, " Neither preaching of the Word withou
nor the dumb chap of his conscience within coul
move him to do weel."

The chapper-up always seemed to me a weir
figure as he shambled hurriedly through the dar
abroad while others slept. Like some ghouli

resurrectionist he disturbed those whom Sleep, " the death of each day's life," had sepulchred, wrenching them back to consciousness that Life might ply its scalpels again upon them.   To those who heard the chapper-up yet need not regard his summons, he must have seemed ominous of the Angel of Death, the Great Chapper-up, whose call to arise and go hence none dare disobey.

When the chapper-up had knocked on pane or window-ledge it was impressive to see a flicker of light appear behind the oblong of gloom, as match was struck or candle lit, proof that the signal had been effectual.   In a Tayside town a chapper-up whose summons invariably banished sleep was irreverently known as " Effectual Calling."

When I have seen the glimmer answer to the knock and a brightness spread behind the dark window I have wondered whether the summons of the Dread Chapper-up, Death, might not likewise have its response in a light beyond the darkness of the grave.

Salads at Dumbarton

I HAVE often wondered why the poets and story-tellers have ignored Dumbarton Rock. Many a minstrel has sung of Snowdoun and many a novelist has told the tales of Dunedin, but ancient Alclyd as dominant as any of the fortress-cliffs which bulwarked Scotland, *caret vate sacro*. Since Ossian passed by and saw the halls of Balclutha that they were desolate, no poet has fashioned even a sonnet in her praise. Though Scott sang of Lennox and Leven Glen, he never brought Dumbarton Castle within the circle of his wizardry, and but permit Jeanie Deans a glimpse of it as she travels to Roseneath. Only the Sassenach, Jane Porter, has chosen the Fort of the Brythons as background for a romantic tale in laying within its ancient wall the scene of one chapter of *The Scottish Chiefs*. Yet few castles have a longer or more romantic record. Is there no Clydesider who will avert his gaze from economics long enough to make the Viking galley moor again under the great rock? Will none re-echo for us the thoughts of the captive Wallace or be pathetic and forecasting over the faring of the girl queen to France from the shore of Dumbarton? Is there no one between the Kilpatrick Hills and Erskine Ferry who will recapture for us the thrill with which we first heard of how Crawford of Jordanhill scaled those dizzy heights and made crash the crumbling wall? St Andrews makes much of having slain two archbishops, in castle and on moor, but Dumbarton hanged one. Why are such deeds hid? What is the good of having a college

at Jordanhill if students cannot recount the exploit
which makes that name sonorous?

I fear, however, we have come too late into a
world too old to hope for *chansons de geste* and
romances that would do fit honour to Dumbarton.
Time is bald behind the ears, and the tresses of
romance adorn his forehead. Yet something of that
middle height which Milton scorned may be achieved
by some lover of Dumbarton with inclinations
towards authorship, even though he seek not to
stand before kings and tell of battles long ago. I
offer him some orra things of history and odds and
ends of human story. Let him brew them with
imagination, and into the cauldron throw descriptions of rock and river, firth and cloud-capt ben,
and Dumbarton may have at last found its novelist.

In 1554 Captain Faucher, a Frenchman attached
to the service of the Regent Mary of Guise, was in
Dumbarton. In the *Balcarres Papers* in the Advocates'
Library, which have been recently published by
The Scottish History Society, there is preserved a
letter which he wrote from Dumbarton to Lady
Livingstone, widow of the fifth Lord Livingstone,
one of the Scots noblemen in attendance on the
girl-queen, Mary Stuart, when she sailed from
Dumbarton to France in 1548. Lord Livingstone
married, in France, Jeanne de Pied de Fer, and one
would like to know something of the ancestor who
first bore that suggestive surname. Lord Livingstone
died in France in 1551, and his widow set off to
see the Scotland which she had never seen as a
wife, and entered the service of Mary of Guise. Her
coming to Scotland raises the presumption that
Lord Livingstone had been kind to her, and the fact
that she was his third wife may be regarded as
confirming the inference. In due time she became
quite a merry widow, for Captain Faucher addresses
his Dumbarton letter to " Madame ma Valentine,

Madame de Levyston." He does not say when or where or why she became his valentine, but my hypothetical novelist will surely make all that clear, remembering how Ophelia babbles of a valentine and how Catherine Glover chose Hal o' the Wynd. He must make Captain Faucher the lover of Lady Livingstone, were it only to prove true the word of Rosalind that the true lover is the most feigning. Captain Faucher is a gallant Frenchman with a pretty skill in phrase, as when he writes, "*je vous avise que j'ay perdu le rire et sans le retour de la Royne ne le saureez recouvrer.*" It is as daintily said as when she who loves Robin Adair sighs, "What's this dull toon to me?" or when the English maiden who cares not to bind her hair laments, "The village seems asleep or dead when Lubin is away." And I am sure that Jeanne de Pied de Fer knew quite well that the return of the Queen was sighed for because it would assure the return of her lady-in-waiting.

Another sentence in the letter will divide all readers into two camps, realists and high-soaring symbolists. "I have found a place where water-cress grows which we may eat as salads, but I know you prefer to eat *la racyne d'alexandre.*" Realists may be right in seeing in this a mere statement of fact. I want to arrange myself with the symbolists and to see in the phrases a plus-quam-Meredithian obscure allusiveness or an esoteric significance such as the Rosicrucians employed. What then does Captain Faucher really mean? The worry of symbolism is that it is susceptible of so many explanations. Hotspur became enraged at Owen Glendower's skimble-skamble stuff of signs and portents, and I confess that even in these days of crossword puzzles I am unable to plumb the depth of Captain Faucher's meaning. Sergeant Buzfuz perverted Mr Pickwick's note about chops and tomato sauce into a declara-

tion of affection, and one is surely justified in
thinking that more is meant than meets the eye in
this talk about salads. Our supposititious novelist
will unravel all, no doubt, and make plain love's
allegories. Let me try a little, however, with this
racyne d'alexandre. Alexanders is a variety of horse-
parsley which was grown in the Middle Ages and
eaten as celery is now. Its name, which appears also
as *alisaundre*, is very puzzling. Some etymologists
assert that " alexanders " is but a perversion
of *olus atrum*, similar to Jerusalem artichoke for
" girasole " artichoke. But the plant is not black,
and the form *alexandre* is found in tenth-century
French. Others argue that as the plant is very
pungent, and was used for flavouring, it was called
" Alexanders " as dominating all other flavours, as
Philip's son conquered the world. If Captain
Faucher knew that theory, he may have been com-
plimenting Lady Livingstone in saying that she ate
only *racyne d'alexandre*, much as Burns wrote:

> O saw ye bonny Lesley?
> She's gane across the Border,
> She's gane like Alexander
> To spread her conquests further.

That explanation may be too direct for a symbolist
who loves a far-fetched meaning. Here then is a
symbolism as complicated as if it were drawn from
Plotinus of the Kabbalah. Alexanders is a parsley.
Parsley was formerly spelled persley, a pronunciation still retained in Scots. Englishmen have changed
persley into parsley, just as they have changed clerk
into clark and Derby into Darby, although none of
the inhabitants of that town would ever say Darby
unless when referring to the great race at Epsom.
The French form is persil, and the Dutch form is
petersile, which shows that French and English
alike have elided a " t," after the fashion of the
Glasgow man who speaks of a " bo'le o' wa'er."

The Dutch is nearest to the Latin petroselinum, under which lies the Greek for rock, since parsley grows on stony ground. Now I think we may begin to see what Captain Faucher means, although he wraps his meaning in as strange symbols as Dr Donne or any of the metaphysical poets. When he says that Lady Livingstone eats only alexanders, he means that she is stony-hearted, or he means that love of her is devouring him, her faithful lover by the great Rock of Dumbarton. If I could only find out that Captain Faucher's Christian name was Alexander, I should feel this last explanation confirmed. But the captain is as mysterious a figure as the Man in the Iron Mask, and his residence in Scotland is as veiled as the exile of Ovid at Tomi.

Charles, Cardinal de Lorraine, writing in 1553 to his sister, Mary of Guise, begs her *bien garder le cappitaine Faucher*, and King Henri II. writes to the same effect. The Cardinal impresses on his sister the necessity of never making mention in her letters of the captain unless when she writes to Madame de Vallentinois, a relative of the Duc de Bouillon. The Cardinal gives as reason for Faucher's banishment that he has *offanse l'admiral et consequammment tout le monde*, and that he has saved the honour of M. de Bouillon. The admiral was that noble Frenchman, Gaspard de Coligny, who perished later on St Bartholomew's Day. I am inclined to put in the wrong anyone who offended Coligny, but probably the Dumbarton novelist will be able to work that in without disadvantage to his hero. He must make Captain Faucher the hero, were it only because he ends his letter so prettily. It sounds best in the antique French, but here is the English of it, " offering myself most humbly to your good graces, and if I am not in them already, praying Our Lord to place and keep me therein, and to give you with good health the fulfilment of all your desires "; *de Dombertrand ce septieme jour de mai par celui qui veult demeurer vostre humble et hobeyssant valentin.* Will not some young enthusiast of Alclyd, who is yet in his salad days, tell me by the magic of imagination something more of these valentines?

This Intolerable Deal of Sack ✎

A Word for the Burns Anniversary

WHEN Prince Hal scans Falstaff's tavern-bill at the Boar's Head, Eastcheap, he exclaims, "O monstrous! but one halfpennyworth of bread to this intolerable deal of sack."

There is a similar disproportion in the study of a poet's poetry as compared with the interest in a poet's life. At the recent Cowper bi-centenary more references were made to his fits of mania than to the characteristics of his poetry. His latest biographer has studied Cowper as "The Stricken Deer" and has given to the consideration of religious experiences, which were not peculiar to Cowper, space which should have been occupied by a study of Cowper's advance from the couplet of Pope to the supple blank verse of *The Task*, to his fresh metrics in *My Mary* and *The Loss of the Royal George*, and to the realism and philosophical depth of *Yardley Oak*.

Wordsworth has received much attention of late, not because men are recognizing "Wordsworth's healing power," or are studying the rhythm of *Laodamia* or are interested in Wordsworth's sonnets as varied from Milton's, or in Wordsworth's odes as passing beyond Gray's, but because Wordsworth's ascetic reputation has been smudged by the revelation of his youthful amour with Annette Vallon.

Literary Edinburgh last summer was divided into two parties regarding the parentage of Sir Walter Scott's wife, a matter of as little significance to

Scott's status as an author as the quarrel of the Bigendians and the Littleendians in Swift's satire. I tested four fierce disputants on their knowledge of Scott as a novelist and a poet by asking them to place Mrs Blower and Nanty Ewart and to repeat Lucy Ashton's song. All failed to pass.

Who reads *Sartor Resartus* now, and what man under fifty could recite Carlyle's rhetoric beginning, " Two men I honour and no third "? But countless smoke-rooms know all about Carlyle's relations with his wife, and are ready to decide whether she threw a tea-cup at him and whether he gave reason for her jealousy of Lady Ashburton.

Mrs Rachel Annand Taylor, an aureate poet herself, seemed a fit interpreter of Dunbar, the master of metres and lover of language. Yet her recent book has an intolerable deal of sack, giving more thought to Dunbar's life and character than to his art in poesy. Just when we are hoping to hear Mrs Taylor explain Dunbar's felicity of phrase, or the sonorous intricacy of his vowel-music, she sets about flyting Dunbar for his " Flytings," for not being a St Francis, though he was a Franciscan, and for being as worldly as Cardinal Beaton, though not so successful.

Instances like these almost justify Matthew Arnold's gibe that literature could not be taught, since a lecturer, professing to treat of the poetry of Shelley, would probably busy himself with " chatter about Harriet." Most books about Shelley do concern themselves more with his erotic extravagance than with the metre of *Adonais*, or the message of *Alastor*. The clash o' the country is a poor substitute for criticism.

What is the proportion between discussion of the life of Burns, which was like that of many of his time, and discussion of his poetry, which was unlike any of his time? An intolerable deal of sack to a halfpennyworth of bread. A lover of Burns should not care who was the father of Anne Park or where the peck o' maut was brewed or what was the text of the sermon Burns heard in the cauld, cauld kirk of Abington. But he should be eager to discover Burns' debt to Ramsay and Fergusson, and even to Hamilton of Gilbertfield, to ponder whether the language of Burns' poems drew anything from the speech of his Mearns father, to study the poet's use of the wheel and the bob in his stanzas and to judge where the device aids and where it impedes, to note the poet's odd syntax in dropping the auxiliary verb and writing " could stown " for " could hae stown," and " could bragged " for " could hae bragged," to trace the loss in rhythmic charm and artistry when Burns added the extra words to the alternate lines of the second version of *Bonnie Doon*, and to pore diligently over the matter and manner, the message and the method of the poet, his language, subjects, sources, style, rhymes, rhythms, teaching. For all of these a lover of poetry cares, and for all of these the details of a poet's life can give neither light nor guidance.

What has a lover of the poet Burns to do with chatter about Mary Campbell or Clarinda? I have often wished that the one had never left Dunoon and that the other had gone with her husband to the West Indies. The poetry of Burns would not have suffered thereby, and some mawkish letters would never have been written.

Study of Burns took the wrong turning at the beginning, and the bad tradition holds of discussing the man, not the poet. One has only to compare Dr Johnson's *Lives of the Poets* with Dr Currie's *Life of Burns* to note the preoccupation of the latter with details of life as compared with the concern of the other with literary achievement. Carlyle's essay goes similarly ajee: he presents Burns as the standardized " great man " whom he admired, not as the great poet. Carlyle knew too little of poetry in Scots to be able to estimate Burns as a poet. Stevenson had skill in analysis of style and was interested in literary technique, but, being " something of the Shorter Catechist," he also diverged to discuss ethics instead of esthetics. Henley, with Henderson, did good work in the sources of Burns, and wrote acutely of the art of Burns. But, as Henley was determined to exalt Burns for what most regarded as his shortcomings, he also wandered into By-Path Meadow. Mrs Carswell goes one better—some would say one worse—than Henley, and can find no fault in the man, with whom she is more concerned than with the poet.

The spate of irrelevance still runs high at every Burns anniversary. Even ministers they hae been kenned to claim Burns as a reformer of the Church's creed, as if *The Holy Fair* were a Moderator's address, or *The Cotter's Saturday Night* a pastoral letter on the decay of revealed religion as described by Professor Crew.

Let us study Burns' poems more, and talk about Burns' life less. The man who laboured at Mossgiel, who shore his hairst at Ellisland, who died prematurely in the Wee Vennel of Dumfries, was in his misfortunes and errors the brother of us all. He was one of the mere men since the Fall who have not been able in this life to keep all the commandments of God. In that likeness to the rest of us there lies no explanation of the immortal memory of Robert Burns. Its explanation lies in his difference from any mere men, from the poet in him, from the poetry of which he was alike the servant and the source.

THE ELUSIVE RIVER

A Roving Survey of the Clyde from Daerhead to the Tail of the Bank

By GEORGE PRATT INSH

Illustrated by A. PENDER CRICHTON, *and with Map End-papers. Crown 8vo. 7s. 6d. net*

THE Clyde in all its varied and challenging aspects—leaping hill-burn, winding watercourse, deep, straight channel for the great liner; the Clyde now harnessed to provide power and illumination for a whole province, now sparkling in the sunshine as it sweeps past trees spangled with the delicate pink of the apple-blossom; the Clyde in winter and in summer, by day and by night; the Clyde constantly revealing, even amid a familiar setting, a new and strange beauty to the eyes of one who has been at all times alert to detect and skilled to interpret its ever-varying appeal; the Clyde thus viewed from an unconventional and highly individualistic standpoint forms the theme of *The Elusive River*, which is written with all the charm and distinction characteristic of the work of Dr George Pratt Insh.

THE FINDHORN

The River of Beauty

By THOMAS HENDERSON

With 16 Illustrations from Pencil Drawings by JOHN CAMERON, *and Map End-papers. 7s. 6d. net*

" A delightful book which should have a wide appeal."
The Glasgow Herald.

" A book composed in a style of charming versatility, making the subject as vivid as the scenes of beauty on the Findhorn. . . . The book is worthy the best in descriptive literature of Scotland."
Scots Observer.

THE MORAY PRESS: EDINBURGH & LONDON

THE AMBER LUTE

Poems from the French translated into Scots

By MARGARET WINEFRIDE SIMPSON

With an Introduction by the

RT. HON. J. RAMSAY MacDONALD

6s. net

To call a poet scholarly suggests immediately that his scholarship exceeds his poetry, but in Miss Simpson we find a happy commingling of the two gifts. The affinity between the Scots and the French people is recognized; in reading Miss Simpson's poems it would be difficult, without her acknowledgment, to suppose that they had sprung from any but a Scots heart.

DAWN TO DUSK

Ventures in Verse

By JOHN HOGBEN

6s. net.

JOHN HOGBEN is the author of, amongst other books, *Richard Holt Hutton of the "Spectator"*; *Shakespeare's Master Passages* and *Wordsworth's Master Passages*. This volume contains verses selected from *The Golf Craze*, *The Highway of Hades*—a book of verse and prose dealing with the Great War—and other earlier works, along with a number of poems hitherto unpublished.

THE ROAD TO THE ISLES

Poetry, Lore and Tradition of the Hebrides

By KENNETH MacLEOD

With an Introduction by MARJORY KENNEDY-FRASER

Crown 8vo. **7s. 6d. net.**

"It is a tribute to Mr MacLeod that one who has never heard more than a word or two of Gaelic spoken, much less sung, may be made, by this book, acutely sensible of his loss."
Times Literary Supplement.

THE MORAY PRESS: EDINBURGH & LONDON